SHRINKING DOLLARS, VANISHING JOBS

SHRINKING DOLLARS, VANISHING JOBS
WHY THE ECONOMY ISN'T WORKING FOR YOU

Dick Cluster/Nancy Rutter
and the staff of Dollars & Sense
magazine

BEACON PRESS   Boston

Grateful acknowledgment is made to Marge Piercy for permission to quote from "Exodus" from *The Twelve-Spoked Wheel Flashing*, published by Alfred A. Knopf, Inc., copyright© 1978, and to Monthly Review Press and Robert Màrquez for permission to quote from "Zero Hour," by Ernesto Cardenal: Copyright© 1974 by Robert Màrquez. Reprinted by permission of Monthly Review Press.

Beacon Press books are published under the auspices
of the Unitarian Universalist Association
Published simultaneously in Canada by
Fitzhenry & Whiteside Limited, Toronto
Printed in the United States of America

(hardcover) 9 8 7 6 5 4 3 2 1
(paperback) 9 8 7 6 5 4 3 2

Library of Congress Cataloging in Publication Data

Cluster, Dick, 1947–
   Shrinking dollars, vanishing jobs.

   Includes bibliographical references.
   1. United States — Economic conditions — 1971–
2. Economic history — 1945–   I. Rutter, Nancy, 1954–   joint
author. II. Dollars & sense (Somerville, Mass.) III. Title.
HC106.7.C58 1980   330.9'73'0926   79–53756
ISBN 0–8070–3200–X
ISBN 0–8070–3201–8

Acknowledgments

Above all, we would like to thank the group members of *Dollars & Sense* for extending the magazine's collective work process to this book and for their help in researching, writing, and talking about the issues and perspectives presented here. Our special thanks go to Frank Ackerman for reading our drafts and for much of the material in chapter seven.

We also wish to thank the Institute for Food and Development Policy for much of the material in chapter six as well as Frank Brodhead, Norm Bowers, and Stephen Weil.

INTRODUCTION: *ANOTHER* BOOK ON ECONOMICS?

ECONOMICS? IT'S THE CLASS you fell asleep in when you were in high school. It's the newscast telling you that something — the cost of wheat, the unemployment rate, the Wholesale Price Index — went up. Again. An economics book? A dull text filled with numbers and tables and explanations that don't make sense.

This isn't a book about economics. It won't tell you how to construct a price index or how to measure the size of the money supply. Those skills may or may not be useful to professors or professional forecasters, but they are patently useless to lay people who are trying to understand the economic forces that are buffeting them.

Nor is this what usually passes for economic reporting: a fifteen-second recitation of the fall of the Index of Leading Indicators, a ten-second quote from an anonymous authority about what this is supposed to mean. Before you can even begin to think about what went down or why, the report is over and it's on to yet another mysterious facet of our economy, the Dow Jones Average of Twenty-six Leading Industrials.

This is a book about the U.S. economy. It describes, in plain English, what decisions are being made, who's making them and why, and what the real-life effect of these decisions is. We take the guesswork out of productivity, unemployment, fiscal policy, the Organization of Petroleum Exporting Countries, and the balance of trade. We talk about them in

terms of working conditions, corporate strategies, family purchasing power, energy needs, and jobs lost or saved.

In particular, the book delves into seven major economic
issues of common concern: those that most directly influence
our everyday lives. The first three chapters revolve around
work: what conditions are found on the job, the reasons
behind unemployment, and the unpaid labor women do in
the home. We discuss why workplaces aren't clean, safe, and
calm; what unions mean to workers; what housework means
to women; and what affirmative action means to blacks. Next,
the book explores the causes and contradictions of big government and the effects of big business on prices and energy
policy. The remaining two chapters describe international
events, which may, on first sight, appear less important than
what goes on in the domestic economy. But the needs and
actions of U.S. corporations around the globe determine the
size of the military budget, the kinds of foreign policy and aid
decisions that are made, and which wars we fight and why.
The competition between these U.S.-based multinational
firms and foreign companies hits home too — it affects the
value of the dollar and the price of imports, determines which
industries do or do not grow, and figures into the timing and
severity of the domestic economy's dips and peaks.

We're presenting a picture of the economy that has come
together over the past five and a half years, through our own
efforts and those of others, in the course of researching and
writing about the economy in an accessible, topical way for
the monthly magazine *Dollars & Sense*. We are not trained
economists, rather we've learned how to use economic
theory and data for the purpose of understanding and explaining what's happening in our society and what needs to
happen.

This way of painting economic realities has proven useful to
many *Dollars & Sense* readers: for community groups,
women's groups and unions, it has provided the kind of clear
analysis and information that make educational and organizing efforts easier and more successful. Others — students,

teachers, houseworkers, wage earners, and retirees — have told us that the combination of straight facts and straight talk allows them to view news reports more critically and make sense out of what doesn't appear to be sensible.

We've applied the same methods to this book. As a result, the book is filled with history and facts — and yes, a large dose of numbers, but it's devoted to depicting the forest, not the trees. It attempts to demystify quite a few examples of economic jargon but always as an aid to understanding a particular problem.

We write from a critical perspective, and we take sides. Our own conclusion, which we expand upon in the final chapter, is that the present system cannot be reformed — it has to be changed. This book, then, is devoted to explaining how the economy works and why it doesn't. We view this as one step toward changing it.

CONTENTS

Introduction: *Another* Book on Economics?   vii

1. Your Job: How It's Structured — and Why   1

2. What Causes Unemployment?   24

3. What *Is* a Woman's Place?   42

4. Government: Big and Getting Bigger   61

5. Monopoly: More Than a Game   82

6. Getting Rich on Foreign Soil   105

7. Trade Wars, or Why Toyota Means More Than Transportation   123

8. Conclusion: Is There an Alternative?   142

   Glossary of Commonly Used Terms   160

   How to Survive: Sources and Resources   168

   Index   175

1.
YOUR JOB: HOW IT'S STRUCTURED — AND WHY

"My father, he knew it was rough. He went through the strike back in the thirties. He went through two of them — when the United Mine Workers first tried to come in here, and then one in about 1932. They made it then; we'll make it now.

"We had one guy got killed right before we went out on strike. Have you ever been in the coal mines? Well, you just couldn't believe it. I tell you, it was bad enough to make us do what we're doing — striking.

"The Mine Enforcement Safety Administration had a toll-free number, but you didn't get caught calling them people. If the company caught you calling the inspectors down there, they'd fire you. They wouldn't come out and say, 'You're fired 'cause you called the inspectors.' They'd fire you for something else. They'd fire you for anything. And with no union, you'd have no say-so whatsoever.

"They say the big thing they don't want to give us in our contract is our safety. It's not the money, it's the safety. They say, 'If we allow you people a safety committee down there at that mine, it's you that'd be controlling the mines instead of us.'

"I think in every twenty-four-hour period, somebody dies in the coal mines. And every month, I believe, there's some seventy-odd people who die in the United States from black lung. So that kills you as sure as if a rock fell on you. But slowly. You can't get no breath and you can't get out;

1

you're all the time taking medicine, oxygen. That's the deaths that people don't see. They say, 'Well, he worked, and he's retired now, got his money... got his benefits.' But what's he doing? He's lying in a house, in a bed, or watching TV. He can't do nothing. So he's a dead man right there.

"The company don't care. It's not their health. If some-body gets hurt, they say they got a stack of applica-tions outside that high, they'll just get somebody else. They're going to make their money — they don't care what this country looks like. All the rivers and creeks polluted. And slate dust burning on the sides of the hills.

"Do I ever think of giving up? No, absolutely not. We were all born and raised here in this county. And nobody is going to come up here and run us off. This is our job.

"We got a job here as long as we want it, for all of our kids and families. And jobs in the future are not going to be all that easy to get. Jobs are getting fewer, not more. And the working people in this country are going to have to start fighting a little bit harder. 'Cause if they don't, they're going to wake up some morning and they won't have a job.

"And a big rich company man, he's going to live — they got their mansions and their ranches and their farms and whatnot. They live inside their gates and they don't care what goes on outside. They're going to pay their workers enough to keep them alive and keep them a little shack to live in.

"But this coal here was put in the ground for all of us. Not just for a few rich people down in Knoxville or up in Michigan or wherever they live. It was put here for all of us. We're all going to get something out of it. And our part of it's not going to be three dollars a day and living on the side of some hill in a little bitty wooden shack. No. It used to be that way, but it ain't going to be that way anymore. 'Cause we deserve more than that.

"We go down there and get it out. Die for it. It's worth more to us than that."

—Phil Tucker, coal miner, on strike for United Mine Workers contract, Whitley City, Kentucky, 1974 (Interview by Liberation News Service)

Poisoned Productivity

Day after day, nearly a hundred million Americans get up in the morning — or the evening — walk out the door and go to work. They mine the coal, keep the books, teach the children, drive the trucks, plow the fields, sell the food. Some love their work; some hate it; many are glad just to have it. Whatever the job or the sentiments, work is at the heart of the economy. Economics can be a dismal science of numbers, even Greek-letter formulas. But for miner Phil Tucker, like most people, pages of economic equations don't add up to much. The formulas used to measure industrial productivity don't affect his knowledge that the machines that increase output also fill the mines with dust. The calculations of the cost of getting a ton of coal out of the ground don't assign a value to a scarred lung or a polluted creek. But to really talk about the economics of work, nothing is more basic than understanding how the job gets done.

In today's economy, a bewildering number of workplaces are so hazardous to workers' health that the jobs, like a pack of cigarettes, ought to carry a warning. In 1977, there were 5,460,000 "reportable" cases of occupational illness and injury for full-time workers in private industry, causing more than 36 million lost working days. A reportable incident, according to the federal Bureau of Labor Statistics, is one that causes death or loss of consciousness or requires medical treatment. A minor accident, a chronic cough, fatigue or tension not treated by a doctor aren't considered serious enough to be reportable.

The types of health hazards produced in America's workplaces are as varied as the new car models the Big Three give us each year. In 1977, the Bureau of Labor Statistics categorized the types of dangers. Lung disease caused by dust, for instance — whether coal dust or cotton dust — accounted for 1.2 percent of all occupational illness and injury cases.

Workers contracting job-related skin disorders accounted for 45.1 percent of the reportable cases in 1977; illnesses resulting from toxic chemicals, poisons, and other physical "agents" were responsible for another 26 percent. Lead, for instance, is an industrial "agent" that threatens the health of workers in at least 125 job categories in industries including auto, rubber, paint, steel, and electronics. Of the remaining workplace hazards, one of the most common is noise. Excessive noise, often overlooked as a serious hazard, threatens the hearing of an estimated 25 million workers in settings that range from disco nightclubs to printing pressrooms.

Constant high levels of noise affect workers even in so-called safe jobs like clerical work. Offices filled with humming, clicking, and buzzing machines and ringing phones have made noise one of the biggest sources of health problems among clerical employees. Noise in an office produces such illnesses as chronic headaches, high blood pressure, emotional stress, and loss of hearing. These noise-related health problems are often compounded by other office hazards. Inadequate or glaring lighting, fumes from office machinery fluids, and fiberglass particles from air conditioners add eyestrain, coughs, and throat irritations to the sicknesses common among office workers.

Industry's response to the problem of workplace health and safety has been characterized by former United Auto Workers (UAW) president Leonard Woodcock as "fix the worker, not the workplace." Requiring employees to wear earmuffs or respirators, it seems, is much cheaper than making engineering changes. So is barring the most vulnerable workers from particular jobs; women of child-bearing age and blacks have been restricted by employers from certain jobs in industries using lead. Exposure to lead is known to cause still births and miscarriages and to result in a high incidence of lead poisoning among blacks with the sickle-cell anemia trait. Job discrimination against a few groups, though, doesn't eliminate the dangers that all workers face in lead industries.

Yet technically, the engineering changes needed to make jobs safer are often quite feasible. In the case of noise, the Occupational Safety and Health Administration (OSHA) has estimated that — political and cost considerations aside — it would take only three years to bring 92 percent of the nation's workplaces down to the noise level of eighty-five decibels proposed by the Environmental Protection Agency (EPA). Nonetheless, it's doubtful that such a safe level will be reached: the present noise standard, some three times higher than that proposed by the EPA, is not rigorously enforced. OSHA receives more protest mail from business on the question of noise levels than on any other form of regulation.

On occasion, engineering changes have been won through workers' collective action. A Chicago area UAW local, for example, succeeded in writing thirteen specific noise-control provisions into its October 1977 contract covering a Ford stamping plant. A Boston United Electrical Workers local walked off the job to protest having to wear earmuffs, forcing management to make engineering changes in the plant instead.

The most dramatic conflict over health and safety on the job is the one carried on, unceasingly, in the coal mines. The danger of sudden cave-ins and explosions is matched by the sure, steady build-up of coal dust in the lungs. The situation of those who, like Phil Tucker, mine the nation's coal reveals a lot about the economics of safety: why increasing productivity makes work more dangerous; why those who don't lose a limb or their lives may lose their jobs; and how unionization helps, or doesn't help, to improve conditions on the job.

Gone Are the Days?

For 110 days in the winter of 1977–78, the United Mine

Workers were out on strike. This, the longest coal strike in recent U.S. history, took place in one of the coldest, most destructive winters in years. There were floods and drought in California, ice storms in the Midwest, and back-to-back blizzards in the Northeast. Utility companies predicted that dwindling coal supplies would bring power shortages; in Washington administration and congressional leaders huddled over plans for seizing the mines. Still the miners rejected two different contract offers and accepted the third only by a 57 percent majority.

The strike revolved around what even the *New York Times,* not particularly sympathetic to the miners, referred to as "givebacks" and "takeaways" — attempts by the coal companies to cancel gains the UMW had won in the past. The most important of these gains was in the area of health and safety. Specifically, the operators wanted to freely fire wildcat strikers, reduce the time spent training new miners, and limit the power of union safety committees in the mines. (Wildcat strikes — that is, locally initiated strikes around specific grievances, as distinguished from national strikes called by union officials at contract time — are an essential tool for protesting dangerous working conditions in the coalfields.) The mine owners also wanted to replace the union-controlled system of free medical clinics with conventional private health insurance plans to which each worker would have to contribute $700 a year.

The history of the strike is best begun three decades back, when coal production in the United States began to drop. Through World War II, coal had been widely used by the railroads and for heating homes. As oil and gas replaced coal in homes, and diesel and electric trains and gasoline-powered trucks and buses took over transportation, coal use declined. Production fell from 631 million tons in 1947 to only 403 million tons in 1961.

To maintain their profits in the face of dwindling sales, coal operators concentrated on maximizing productivity — on getting more coal out of fewer workers through mechanization. One aspect of this drive was the shift to strip mining, but the application of new machines to underground mining was equally important. Into the deep mines came the Continuous Miner, a machine that literally chews into a mine wall with a scoop equipped with teeth. Side shovels scrape up the dug-away coal and put it into buckets on a conveyor belt that hauls the coal above ground.

The operators' strategy succeeded. Productivity rose from 6.4 tons per miner per day in 1947 to 13.9 in 1961. While production fell by one-third, employment fell by two-thirds. Even after coal output began to rise again in the early 1960s (as increased demand from electric companies brought about a coal revival), employment continued to decline throughout the decade. When the song "Sixteen Tons" was recorded in the early fifties, it described more than twice what a miner could really produce in a day; in the sixties, it was an average day's work.

Union officialdom went along with this trend, choosing to sacrifice some members and provide well for those who re-mained. The UMW actually lent money to big companies to finance mechanization. The miners who retained their jobs enjoyed rising real wages; their weekly pay rose 2.2 percent a year faster than the rate of inflation from 1947 to 1969. They also won, in 1950, the free medical system, financed by a per-ton royalty payment from the operators. This system, the best in the country, provided hospital, nursing home, and psychiatric services as well as a network of clinics empha-sizing continuous health supervision, early disease detection, and preventive care.

Not only did mechanization spell unemployment, poverty, and environmental destruction for many coal-producing areas, but the human costs of coal remained high. The faster pace of work accompanying mechanization made coal mining more dangerous, not less so. Death and injury rates on the job, worse than in any other industry, were actually higher in 1969 than in 1949. (These figures, as well as the productivity ones cited above, include the supposedly safer

strip mines as well as those underground.) Also, many observers believe that the Continuous Miner and similar
machinery created more dust than the old methods, thereby
increasing the incidence of black lung.

In 1969, things started to turn around in the coal industry.
Productivity (output per miner) has been declining since that
year, and employment has steadily risen. The death rate in
the mines has dropped sharply.

The connections are far from coincidental. They stem from
the emergence in the Appalachian coal towns of a grass-roots
movement protesting the unsafe conditions in the mines, the
plight of former miners disabled by black lung, and the cor-
ruption and unresponsiveness that had set in among UMW
leadership.

This movement is best known for ousting UMW president
Tony Boyle in a government-supervised election in 1972,
after Boyle's hired assassins had killed previous opposition
candidate Jock Yablonski. But miners and their families had
been causing difficulties for the mine owners for some years
beforehand and all of these difficulties cut into productivity.

First, there was a rapid rise in wildcat strikes, often related
to safety problems. The number of strikes in the coal industry
grew from 207 in 1967 to 1,039 in 1973; strike-bound mines
meant less production per worker. Second, in 1969, pressure
on Congress led to the passage of the Coal Mine Health and
Safety Act, which required companies to hire many more
workers for maintenance, ventilation, dust control, and other
activities that do not increase the output but do make mines
safer. Legislation requiring reclamation of strip-mined land
had a similar effect. Finally, the contract negotiated in 1974
by the new president, Arnold Miller (and subject, for the first
time, to ratification by the rank and file) included a number of
important safety measures: any miner could now withdraw
from an unsafe area, even against a foreman's order; more
training was required for new miners; and 7,000 new jobs
were created for full-time helpers on dangerous jobs.

Meanwhile, real wages continued to rise. Ordinarily, the

combination of rising wages and falling productivity would add up to a squeeze on profits. The coal companies were saved from that fate, however, by the energy crisis. Electric utilities are the principal buyers of coal; as the price that utilities pay for for oil, gas, or nuclear power has gone up, coal companies (many of which are owned by oil companies anyway) have been able to raise their prices without losing customers. Between 1969 and 1976, the price of coal went up two and a half times as fast as average consumer prices. The share of coal revenue going to wages actually dropped from 35 percent in 1969 to 23 percent in 1976.

Nonetheless, in 1977, the coal companies felt that the time had come to act. One factor often cited by analysts of the industry was the union's growing weakness as the operators turned to Western, nonunion mines. Possibly they also feared the future effect of new, tighter federal safety standards adopted in 1977. (Said the public relations director of the Bituminous Coal Operators' Association, "'Tighter' sounds like they're good. They're more bothersome.") Also it is likely that they saw 1977 as a year when the union and the grass-roots miners' movement were in disarray. The Miners for Democracy movement that had put Miller in office no longer existed, rank-and-file dissatisfaction with what Miller had been able to accomplish was growing and officials from the old union regime were jockeying for position as well.

Furthermore, the union-controlled clinic system, financed as it was on the basis of per-ton rather than per-worker payments by the coal company, was bankrupted by falling productivity and soaring medical costs. The companies wanted to scrap it rather than reorganize it.

Whatever the operators' strategy, they underestimated the resistance they would meet. "Gone are the days when a coal walkout could send shivers through the economy and move Presidents to take over the mines," gloated *U.S. News & World Report* as the strike began, but the miners surprised everyone. They rejected, not only the mine owners' first offer, but a compromise contract advocated by their union officials as well. The strike continued almost without formal organization, but with widespread support and donations of food and money from other unions and rank-and-file groups across the country.

The end result was a contract that retained the language of the previous one on almost all safety-related questions. Private health insurance plans, established separately by each coal company, did replace the union-run system, but the miners' contributions were reduced from the proposed $700 to $200 a year. Only slight progress was made on pensions, which had been another bone of contention.

Ever-increasing demands for improved conditions in the mines are sure to plague coal mine owners in the future, and labor militance has been a tradition in the coal fields for over half a century. The 110 days in the winter of 1977–78 were one more round in the continual rematch over the way in which the country's coal is brought out of the ground.

The Same Story Above Ground

Boosting output-per-worker by changing the way people work is hardly a practice limited to mining; it has been a favorite tactic in many businesses since the turn of the century. Methods of "scientific management" — designed to cut production and labor costs by controlling every phase of a work process — caught on in American industry in the 1890s and have held on ever since. Time-and-motion studies carried out by specially trained stopwatch-carrying observers break down each activity into the smallest possible component parts, each with a strict performance-time allotment. Workers are given rigidly defined jobs — tightening a bolt, sewing a seam — as the doing is separated from the thinking. The thinking, the understanding of a job, is centralized in the managers and engineers; labor costs are cut by reducing the training and skill requirements of workers. And piecework and quota systems are designed to draw the maximum production out of each employee. The more recent trends of mechanization and automation, which tie the worker not only to the pace and plan set by the supervisor but also to the pace and plan of the machine, are merely the modern extension of this process.

Vital to employers — whether in steel or retail trade, newspaper printing or coal mining — is their employees' productivity. Workers' performance in an industry is measured by a productivity index — the output of an industry divided by the total number of hours worked by all employees. Higher productivity is one of those national goals we are all supposed to be pursuing, like a strong national defense and, for that matter, the elimination of waxy build-up on our kitchen floors. But the truth is that higher productivity is a national goal because it's an essential ingredient of higher profits, with results for the worker that are just as likely to be disastrous as delightful. The calculation of vacation time in a productivity index provides a telling example of whose welfare is measured by productivity figures. The numbers used for total-worker-hours usually include paid vacation time, since from a business point of view what matters is output as compared to labor *costs*. The more vacation time workers in a given industry or company get, the lower the productivity figure.

The steel industry managed to speed up production to the point where the number of worker-hours required to produce a fixed amount of steel declined by 25 percent between 1960 and 1975. This may have been good news for U.S. Steel, but steelworkers experienced a doubling of injury rates between 1961 and 1969. And between 1960 and 1974 (the year *before* recession caused big layoffs in the steel industry), total employment in blast furnaces and steel mills dropped from 528,000 to 487,000, whereas total production increased.

What's true in the heat of the blast furnace can be true in the air-conditioned office as well. White collar and service work have been growing faster than factory jobs for some time, and the increasing wage bills have brought greater concern about productivity in these fields as well. Medical lab technicians rarely carry out their own tests today; they operate testing machines, which must be fixed by still other technicians when they break down: fast-food workers transfer packaged items from freezer to frialator.

The shift away from factory work is not as rapid as some commentators imply. From 1972 to 1978, the number of employed people working as laborers, machine operators, and traditional craftspeople dropped from 34 percent to 33 percent, whereas the number of those working as clericals, technicians, supervisors and administrators, and service workers (waiters, floor cleaners, hospital aides, and so on) grew from 49 percent to 51 percent. The number of professionals showed little change at all. But in terms of where *new* jobs are coming from, the shift is more significant. Operative, laborer, and craft jobs accounted for only 22 percent of the total increase in employment during that period, whereas the clerical, service, technical, and administrative categories accounted for 66 percent.

Clerical work — which today accounts for 18 percent of total employment — is a favorite target of productivity boosters. The first attempts to apply industrial techniques to clerical work were reflected in the appearance of scientific-office-management books early in this century. In *Labor and Monopoly Capital*, Harry Braverman cites a 1960 office managers' handbook presenting results of time-and-motion studies conducted by General Electric and other major corporations. Office workers should be allowed exactly .014 of a minute to open the side drawer of a standard desk, the handbook suggests, and .015 of a minute to close it. Under the heading "chair activity," the corporate guide's standard for the permissible time consumed in turning in a swivel chair is set at .009 of a minute.

As the number of clerical workers has swelled, the office has become a new frontier of mechanization. The modern reorganization of office work is based on computerized recordkeeping and computer typewriters. Computerized data processing reduces the work of bookkeepers, file clerks, and other recordkeepers to the strictly defined task of talking to the computers that will in turn do the thinking. Choosing the right number and hitting the right key are the only skills required. What's more, because computer time is expensive and computers are unable to recognize mistakes, data-processing workers are required to meet ever-stricter standards of speed and accuracy. Time-and-motion studies even become obsolete; a key-puncher's speed and output can be electronically monitored by machine.

Employers encourage employee acceptance of the new procedures with claims that as machines take over routine work office work becomes more interesting. But the fact is that file clerks displaced by computerized office machines rarely get hired for higher-level computer positions, especially if they're women. Studies of office computerization cited by Jean Tepperman in *Not Servants, Not Machines: Office Workers Speak Out!* show that companies usually bring in male computer personnel from outside, while women clericals continue in the low-level data-entry jobs.

What these computers have done for recordkeeping, "word-processing systems" are now slated to do for secretarial work. Typewriters with memories, produced by corporations including IBM and Xerox, store form letters and prepackaged paragraphs and phrases on magnetic cards or tape, typing them out automatically at 160 to 180 words per minute. The typist's job is to stop the machine at intervals to insert names or special information, fed to her or him through a headset connected to a boss's dictation machine.

In its most advanced form, the office of the future eliminates most personal secretaries, consigning all letter production to word-processing centers where each typist responds to a never-ending stream of tape-recorded instructions from remote executives who are referred to, in the humorless jargon of word-processing planners, as "dictators." Word processing, interestingly enough, is meeting resistance not only from clerical workers but from their bosses, who resent being deprived of the status and services that come with having one's own "girl" assigned to one's office. But equipment manufacturers and corporate cost accountants are pushing hard for the new ways. Says an IBM vice president, "People will adapt to office systems — if their arms are broken. And we're in the twisting stage now."

The biggest payoff, for employers, is the opportunity to reduce clerical staffs. At Penn Mutual Life Insurance in Philadelphia, executives from the president on down dictate into the memory bank of a word-processing center. One department head reported he was now able to do without 35 of his former 125 secretaries. The trade magazine *Word Processing* cited an executive of another satisfied company as saying that 6.5 secretaries with magnetic-card typewriters could do the work of 22.5 armed only with standard machines. Studies of other forms of computerization in banks and insurance companies reveal the elimination of a hundred or more clerical jobs at a time.

The conventional wisdom is that the trend toward automation — in heavy industry, at supermarket checkout counters, almost everywhere — is good for the country and good for the workforce. The jobs lost to machines, we're told, are replaced by jobs that upgrade our skills and challenge our intellects, while the increased output of goods and services fattens our Gross National Product and strengthens our economy.

But such wisdom becomes foolishness to those working in automated jobs that are simultaneously nerve-wracking and tedious, lame rationalization for those standing in unemployment lines or retiring with respirators. Technological advances do offer tremendous possibilities for reorganizing work and eliminating menial tasks — but not if those benefits are continually sacrificed on the altar of increased productivity.

Big Labor and Black Progress?

The issue of productivity rarely receives any public attention except when economists are bemoaning a lack of it; workplace safety vanishes from the news except when a major disaster is reported in ghoulish detail. We hear quite a lot, on the other hand, about some other job-related matters, such as what the American Federation of Labor and Congress of Industrial Organizations (AFL-CIO) head George Meany has to say and whether or not the government and private industry are practicing reverse discrimination. This chapter will conclude, therefore, with a look at two of the most prominent myths about work in America: the myth of big labor and the myth of black progress. Both myths are built around real successes by mass movements for social change. But the changes are far from complete, a fact the myths obscure.

Union Membership Slipping

Big labor. Commentators sound off about it, government officials alternately court and chide it. When trucks stop rolling, assembly lines grind to a halt, and coal is not being mined, it's big labor that makes the headlines. And there is such a thing, complete with sizable memberships stretching across the nation and business-suited officials who are called to the White House. Teamsters used to be people who drove horses; now the 400,000 Teamsters are cannery workers, pipeline diggers, reservation clerks, nurses, high school principals, and, of course, truck drivers. Coal miners, as we have just said, can make quite a bit of trouble when the chips are down. But the fact is that union members are a steadily declining share of the workforce. Only one out of five employed people and active job seekers today belongs to a union.

The period of the Great Depression and World War II saw phenomenal growth in unionism, as the great industrial organizing drives swelled union membership from 3 million to 15 million between 1934 and 1947. In manufacturing, mining, construction, transport, and communications, the union became a permanent institution. But since 1947, the total number of union members has grown slowly or, at times, not at all. In recessions, the numbers have actually dropped — for example, from 20.2 million to 19.4 million between 1974 and 1976.

Table 1
Where Are the Unions
and
Where Are the Workers?

Industry	% Unionized	% of Total Employment
Construction	69	4.7
Mining	54	0.9
Manufacturing	46	22.8
Government	21	17.4
Services	13	17.9
Wholesale and retail trade	8	21.8
Finance, insurance, and real estate	1	5.2
Agriculture	unknown	3.7

Source: Bureau of Labor Statistics, Unionization, *Directory of National Unions and Employee Associations, 1975,* and Employment, *Employment & Earnings,* January 1979.

Note: This breakdown is by *industry,* not occupation. Thus clerical workers hired by manufacturing corporations are included as manufacturing employees. The largely nonunion *occupational* category of clerical workers accounts for 17.9 percent of the employed.

Most membership gains made since the 1940s have been automatic, through the growth of employment at firms with union contracts rather than through organizing efforts at nonunion workplaces. This doesn't mean that people are indifferent to unions — throughout the 1970s workers were less likely to quit union jobs than similar nonunion ones. Rather, the slow growth has to do with the stagnation and even decline of employment in the industries and the regions that are unions' strongholds.

Between 1965 and 1978, for instance, the number of jobs in manufacturing grew by only 2 million, whereas service industries (health, food service, entertainment, etc.) added 7 million jobs and wholesale and retail trade added 6.5 million. Table 1 shows the pattern of employment by industries, compared to their percentages of unionization.

Unions have made some inroads into the growing industries. Many retail workers, especially grocery store chain workers, have unionized. Government workers have also won union protection. But the overall percentage of union membership has dropped. In 1958, 24.2 percent of the labor force was unionized. By 1976, that figure had dropped to 20.1 percent. These numbers somewhat understate unions' influence, since the total labor force includes many of the unemployed, the self-employed, unpaid family workers, and other categories unlikely to join unions; these figures also do not count members of employee associations (common among public employees) as unionists, even when the associations engage in collective bargaining. Union and association members made up 28.3 percent of paid employees in nonagricultural workplaces in 1976, down from 30 percent in 1970.

Another contributor to the downward trend has been the runaway shop: the company that flees its old location in search of a warmer business climate. Between 1967 and 1976, the nation's old industrial heartland — the area north of the Ohio and Potomac rivers and east of the Mississippi — lost 1.5 million manufacturing jobs (more than likely union jobs). In the same period, the states of the South and Southwest gained more than 900,000. As an executive of the Fantus Corporation, a consulting firm specializing in plant relocation, told an Ohio newspaper in 1977, "Labor costs are the big thing. Nine out of ten times you can hang [a company move] on labor costs and unionization."

A unionized General Motors unit that moved to a new nonunion plant in Louisiana, for instance, was able to reduce wages by $2.00 an hour. In 1974, the percentage of unionized nonfarm employees in the Sunbelt ranged from a low of 7 percent in North Carolina to a high of 19 percent in Alabama, compared to a national average of 26 percent. Eleven states in the South and Southwest offer employers legislative protection against unions, in the form of "right-to-work" laws forbidding union shops — workplaces where new employees automatically become union members.

The giant textile firm J. P. Stevens typifies this attempt to beat unions by running away. Stevens, which once operated 98 different mills in the Northeast, is now an entirely Southern company. It employs 7 percent of the South's 689,000 textile workers, concentrated in the "right-to-work" states of North and South Carolina. In 1978, for instance, the average hourly pay rate for manufacturing employees in North Carolina was $4.53; nationwide, manufacturing workers averaged $6.16 per hour. The company has routinely fired pro-union employees and refused to negotiate with unions. Stevens has calculated that it is cheaper to violate labor laws and pay an occasional fine or back-pay settlement than to recognize a union. "The law just isn't designed to handle situations like Stevens," one exasperated National Labor Relations Board lawyer confessed. "They've just smiled and put the knife to their employees."

Backed up by a nationwide boycott campaign against Stevens' products, workers in the company's seven Roanoke Rapids, North Carolina, plants are continuing to hold out for recognition of the Amalgamated Clothing and Textile Workers Union local they chose in a dramatic August 1974 election. To date, Stevens has refused to recognize the union. An important strength of the Stevens struggle has been a remarkable unity between white and black workers, which casts a hopeful light on the Southern union picture. As local union leader Alice Tanner told a 1,000-strong rally a year after the successful vote, "The company don't like you black or white. All they want is your green."

Since New Deal days, unions have depended on the political power stemming from their alliance with the Democratic Party to enhance their influence. Higher minimum wages, workplace health and safety provisions, public works programs and other forms of job-creating stimulation of the economy all have been won in Congress rather than at the bargaining table, and all have benefited nonunion and unionized workers alike. But the slow pace of union organizing is now reflected in weakness in the legislative arena as well.

Manufacturing Jobs, Lost and Gained, 1967–76

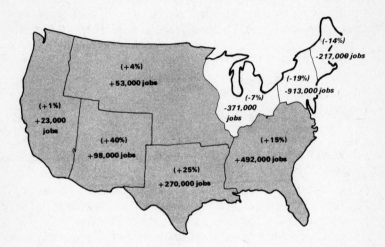

With the election of a Democratic president and Congress in 1976, the major unions expected significant legislative gains. Among them was to be a revised National Labor Relations Act imposing stiffer penalties on companies like J. P. Stevens that interfere with legal organizing efforts: despite one of the best-financed and most sophisticated lobbying efforts ever launched by the AFL-CIO, the bill was defeated. A construction site picketing bill was also defeated, minimum wage and full employment bills were drastically watered down, and national health insurance failed to make it to the floor of either House.

The future of the unions largely depends on their ability to penetrate the new sectors and the runaway shop regions. In the past, entire nonunion industries have been rapidly transformed into union ones in great spurts of organizing associated with the introduction of a qualitatively different kind of unionism. The industrial unionism of the 1930s and 1940s swept mass production industries where craft unionism had failed for decades: the mobilization of large numbers of new activists buttressed labor's political strength as well. To do the same thing for the unorganized sectors today could require a similar leap based on a new approach to workers' problems. One important part of such an approach would have to be increased attention to the needs of the rapidly growing numbers of female workers in the nonunion industries (see chapter three).

Progress with the Brakes On

The civil rights movement was the biggest social movement to arise in America since the union movement of the 1930s, and it gave birth to all the other struggles of the 1960s. On the employment front, it succeeded in outlawing the racial discrimination that had been practiced here since before the founding of the nation, and it even secured the acceptance of the unprecedented corrective principle of affirmative action.

Most simply put, affirmative action means no longer relying on companies' promises not to discriminate against individuals in the future, but instead enforcing hiring patterns that will give all groups equal shares of the jobs in proportion to their numbers and the availability for work. Ignoring the legal double talk about the difference between a goal, a quota, and a timetable, affirmative action means requiring companies to find, train, hire, promote, and pay equal wages to specified numbers of qualified applicants from groups against whom they have discriminated in the past.

Affirmative action is unpopular with business because it brings outside interference in hiring and firing decisions, usually jealously guarded as management prerogatives. In 1976, *Fortune* magazine claimed that the Civil Rights Act of 1964 had "to a considerable extent succeeded," but the federal Equal Employment Opportunity Commission had "perverted its mission" by encouraging preferential hiring through a "confrontationist assault" on private business. The

magazine challenged the government to confront the question of "whether it will be permitted to continue doing so."
And some white workers, having a hard time getting by despite their historically privileged position, have brought suit
against affirmative action regulations that they feel stack the
deck against them. After all the years of black progress since
the Civil Rights Act is it really necessary to maintain admin-
istratively cumbersome and politically ticklish programs to
encourage minority hiring?

The answer provided by a statistical survey of the position
of black America is an emphatic yes. Changes in the access
to jobs are reflected in Table 2. Nonwhites remain overrepresented in lower paid, lower status jobs. (The census category
"nonwhite" is made up of about 90 percent blacks and 10
percent Asians and Native American peoples.) Despite much-
publicized advances in professional fields, the big story between 1964 and 1973 was the number of nonwhites who left
farm labor and domestic service and got jobs in manufacturing. This dramatic rise in factory work stopped dead in the
1974–75 recession. In the important category of unionized
heavy industry (in Table 2, roughly represented by the "durable goods manufacturing" line) large layoffs actually reversed the trend; even by 1978, nonwhites had not regained
the place they won in 1973.

Progress toward equality in other higher-paying occupations has been slow. The major motion in recent years seems
to be in the top professions. The percentage of nonwhites employed as architects, engineers, lawyers, doctors, dentists,
scientists, professors, artists, and entertainers climbed from
4.9 percent to 7.5 percent between 1972 and 1978. But the
gains in this elite category are by definition limited to small
numbers of people. The 341,000 nonwhites employed in
these occupations in 1978 accounted for only 3.2 percent of
all nonwhite jobholders. And even with their rapid entrance
into these professions, blacks are still underrepresented there.
The only large professional fields where nonwhites are employed in nearly the same proportion as in the workforce as a

Table 2
Percent of Jobs Held by Nonwhites

Occupation	1964	1973	1975	1978
All occupations	10.7	10.8	10.7	11.2
Professionals and technicians	6	8	8	9
Managers and administrators	3	4	4	5
Salespeople — wholesale	2	3	3	4
Salespeople — retail	3	5	6	6
Clerical workers	5	9	9	11
Skilled craftsworkers	6	7	7	7
Machine operatives (nontransport)	11	14	14	15
In durable goods manufacturing	9	16	13	14
Vehicle drivers	13	15	14	15
Laborers	27	20	19	18
Paid household workers	49	39	39	33
Service workers	20	18	18	19

Source: Bureau of the Census, "Current Population Survey." (Based on samples, not an actual census).

Note: Though nonwhites held a higher percentage of the jobs in 1978 than previously, the gap between black and white employment rates also widened. In other words, blacks were a growing proportion of the entire labor force, and they were entering the labor force in search of work much faster than they were finding jobs.

whole are nursing and elementary school teaching. Teaching, a traditional avenue of upward mobility, is not providing many new jobs because of dwindling post–baby boom enrollments, and budget cuts. Among smaller professions, the main cases where nonwhites are statistically overrepresented are the jobs that involve serving as government or corporate ambassadors to their own people — social workers, personnel specialists, vocational and educational counselors. All in all, the unemployment rate for black college graduates in 1977 (6 percent) was only slightly lower than that for whites who had merely finished high school (7 percent).

In terms of family incomes, blacks are now falling behind whites. All through the 1960s, black family incomes grew faster than those of whites, though they still remained nearly 40 percent lower. But this gain was stopped in the 1970s, and in the years 1976 and 1977, while much of America was recovering to some degree from the recession, blacks were left out. Between 1975 and 1977, median white family income grew 17 percent (to $16,740) while prices grew 13 percent; thus white families managed to get slightly ahead. Black families saw their median income grow only 9 percent (to $9,563), falling well behind the rate of price increases.

It is impossible to identify the causes of this decline — to determine what combination of an increasingly stagnant economy and the decline of an organized black protest movement is at work. But it's clear that removing the limited protection provided by affirmative action programs, at this point, would be asking for a return to conditions of the pre–civil rights movement days.

2.
WHAT CAUSES UNEMPLOYMENT?

June 1, 1979, was a raw gray day in Boston. A cold ocean breeze whipped across the concrete plaza in front of the fortresslike Charles F. Hurley state office building. The steady stream of people leaving the building walked briskly, yet they were willing to stop and talk with us about what had brought them down to the city's classic 1960s-urban-renewal government district on that unseasonable morning.

They were young and old; balding and long-haired; black, white, Hispanic, Chinese; clothed in suits, dresses, and blue jeans. Still, they all had one thing in common. They were unemployed. They had just come from the biweekly ritual of signing their names and picking up their unemployment compensation checks. Their stories tell another story about work in America — one that's never too far from the minds of most working people, employed or not.

"This is my twenty-fifth week," said a retail sales worker. "The outfit I worked for just went under and I can't find another opening. The economy's run down, money is tight, so retailing suffers. Twenty-four years I worked straight — I've never been unemployed like this before. I put in a lot more than they're gonna give me back too — that's for sure."

A bookkeeper said: "I had a great job, but the job —

actually the company — relocated to another state. Their home office was there, and they had to find ways to save money, so they just phased us out; they're going to do all their business from that one office now. I've been looking for another job, but most of them don't pay what I need. They want to start you at the bottom, and I feel like I've had too much experience, put in too much time, to start all over again."

"I've been out a month," said a hotel housekeeper. "I was at the Washingtonian, but things weren't going right. Prejudice; a lot of lies were being told, so I just quit. I'd take mill work, or a cooking job, too, but everywhere I go they say they don't need anybody. There are jobs around, but most places I go they just look at your skin and that's it."

"I'm out of work every winter, my work is seasonal," said a construction plasterer. "But I'm usually back at work by now. Slower this year, and they're hiring the younger guys first; I'm sixty-four. Been doing this for forty years, too, don't know what I'll do if housing doesn't pick up. Course, I can see why it's slow. I don't know who can afford to pay the price for houses these days. Who can afford to buy a home for a hundred and twenty-five thousand dollars?"

"I've been out since last October and it's horrible. I'm climbing the walls," said a truck driver. "The company closed up and left forty of us high and dry. I've been looking in my line, in all kinds of lines actually, but there just isn't anything that pays enough to keep my family going. I'm a Teamster, Local Eighty-two, but all the companies in my local aren't doing any business, so the union can't help me out. The worst of it is, this is my last check I just picked up; I don't know what I'll do now. After working thirty years and never collecting, they just say, 'No extension,' just like that. I just don't know what I'll do next."

In June 1979, the official rate of unemployment in the nation stood at 6.0 percent. In other words, according to government statistics, 6.2 million people out of a labor force of 104 million (including all workers over sixteen years old) were looking for work but were unable to find it.

The government describes a period when the unemployment rate drops to 4 percent as a period of *full* employment. Supposedly, if joblessness were to drop further, there would be a serious shortage of workers in important fields. To call a time when more than 4 million can't find work a period of full employment is nonsense, but the dispute over terminology is fast becoming irrelevant anyway. The fact is that the economy hasn't functioned at a 4-percent unemployment level at any time in the past decade.

Unemployment ranged between 4 and 6 percent during the opening years of the 1970s, but zoomed up to 9 percent in the worst months of the 1974–75 recession — a level unseen since the Great Depression. It didn't drop back below 6 percent until June 1978. Even the definition of *prosperity* seems to be undergoing quite a change. Back in 1958, the Eisenhower Administration faced a major crisis when widespread layoffs pushed the unemployment rate up to 6.8 percent. Yet in 1977, the Carter Administration was patting itself on the back for its success in getting the rate "down" to 7 percent.

The problem of unemployment becomes all the more serious if we look at what is behind the Labor Department statistics. The numbers reported each month by the news media seriously understate the number of Americans out of work. The real level of unemployment is at least one and a half times the official rate, and probably double it.

The hitch has to do with determining who should be counted as unemployed. The federal statisticians exclude two significant categories of people: part-time workers who would prefer full-time work but can't find it, and people who want to work but have become so discouraged about finding satisfactory steady jobs that they've given up actively searching.

Part-time workers are counted among the employed exactly as if they were full-time employees. Yet the government's own surveys show that over the past few years, a third to a sixth of the 17 million part-time workers wanted more work but were unable to find it. Each of them should be counted as only half employed. Discouraged workers, excluded from the labor force entirely by the statisticians, are harder to count. Private studies based on detailed interviews suggest that there are at least half as many discouraged workers as there are officially recognized active job seekers. So all told, the *real* unemployment rate on that 1979 spring day in Boston was probably somewhere between 8.5 percent and 12 percent.

Last in the Labor Department press releases, but first if you're trying to figure out who is affected most by unemployment, come the figures showing that some groups and areas are much harder hit than others. Many large cities, and even whole states, experience unemployment rates significantly higher than average. In 1978, for instance, the official rates for New York, Alaska, and the District of Columbia were more than 7.5 percent, as compared to the national figure of 6 percent.

The official unemployment rate for women is usually about two percentage points higher than that for men. This added difficulty in finding a job is most painfully felt by the one in seven families that is headed by a woman alone. But even among two-parent families, a growing number require two wage earners. Since the late 1960s, wages have been in a seesaw battle with prices. Real wages — that is, what a paycheck will actually buy — are no higher than they were in 1967; and they're lower than they have been at some point in between. The only way the average family can improve its purchasing power is to add a wage earner.

For minority groups and teen-agers, the unemployment figure is bleaker still. Nonwhite workers are almost twice as likely as whites to be out of work, according to the official figures. Teen-agers, with least experience and least seniority, are also last hired, first fired. In June 1979, the *official* unemployment for blacks aged sixteen to nineteen was 45 percent; for Hispanic teen-agers it was 21 percent; and for whites of the same age the rate was 16 percent. It has been said that a whole generation of inner-city youth is growing up without the experience of holding a steady job. One newspaper columnist who went to interview Hispanic young people in New York City's South Bronx in 1978 was immediately surrounded by kids offering their names in the hope of getting jobs, simply because he took a notebook out of his pocket.

The Roller-Coaster Economy

Where have the jobs gone? Here is a society that prides itself on being the richest on earth, the world's leader in production, one that teaches its members to value individual initiative and earning money above all other things. Yet it is never able to provide every citizen with a job, and it experiences periodic recessions and depressions in which millions of supposedly secure workers have the rug pulled out from under them. At times in the past decade more than a quarter of the nation's industrial capacity has been unused. Why?

As government and corporate spokespeople keep reminding us, the responsibility for providing jobs in a free enterprise system falls primarily on private business. Private companies employ four fifths of the workers in the economy. Yet when these companies look over their balance sheets and make the decisions that determine the direction of the economy, the number of people they employ is not the "bottom line."

The bottom line is profits, and the prospects of reinvesting those profits to make still more profits. The work ethic may be — or may once have been — the basis of our culture, but the profit ethic is the basis of our economy. How many people will be able to get jobs depends on two major decisions by business: how much to produce and how to produce it. If businesses do not maintain or expand their level of production, there will not be enough jobs. If they choose to expand production but they do it in such a way that they need fewer workers to get the work done, again there won't be enough jobs.

Workplace automation, on-the-job speedup, new methods of supervision, and the threat or reality of runaway shops are all quite efficient in allowing employers to produce their products at a lower cost. They are not so efficient, though, at making work safe or satisfying, saving energy, encouraging cooperation among workers — or providing jobs.

The question of *whether* companies will produce is associated with the more mysterious boom-and-bust roller coaster that economists refer to, colorlessly, as the business cycle. Though talk of expansion, recession, recovery, slump, overheating, cooling off, and similar terms more and more dominates the nightly news, the fractured and mystified way the cycle is presented leaves it as murky to most Americans as the difference between a Republican and a Democrat.

The American experience with economic booms and busts is nothing new. The Panic of 1837 unseated President Martin Van Buren, the panics of 1873 and 1893 were the dark side of the country's Gilded Age, and the Great Depression of the 1930s gave rise to the new economic policies of Franklin Roosevelt. Those policies, though, didn't really end the depression — World War II did. Roosevelt's policies had less to do with the huge drop in the nation's unemployment rate — from 17 percent in 1939 to only 2 percent by 1944 — than did the wartime economy's need for manpower.

But the business cycle is no mere historical curiosity. Panics and depressions have been replaced by recessions and slowdowns, and even (thanks to an anonymous speechwriter in the Ford Administration) sideways waffles. Still, since World War II we've been through a half dozen periods of recession, followed by an equal number of recoveries. The economics textbook definition of *recession* these days is "a time when the value of the nation's total output of goods and services, corrected for inflation, declines for two three-month periods in a row." Recessions are *not* defined in terms of unemployment. The key gauge is businesses' *income* from selling goods and services, *not* the unemployment level.

Why does this income ever decline? Because at various times businesses find that it is not profitable to produce more. This situation is the result of a complex web of factors, none of which has to do with whether or not the country needs the goods, services, and jobs in question.

Three crucial strands of this web are the strength of workers in their efforts to win better pay and working conditions; the ability of consumers to pay for products and services; and the economic outlook regarding international competition, inflation and other current trends. As a result of these factors, individual businesses may decide not to produce now, but instead to wait until the time is right. Though recessions bring temporary damage to firms' profits and sometimes drive smaller companies out of business, they create a climate for a very profitable recovery later on. The three major factors are worth a closer look:

1. Wage squeeze. The closer the economy gets to full employment, the better position employees are in vis-à-vis their employers. This is particularly true of unionized workers, but to one degree or another it is true of everyone. Whether it is a question of going out on strike, threatening to quit, or simply slowing down to a manageable pace, you're in better shape if you've accumulated some savings from working steadily, if there aren't a lot of unemployed people clamoring for your job, and if you can find another job when you need to.

These advantages, for workers, of a high employment period are a major reason why no business expansion goes on forever. Whenever the economy picks up steam (that is, whenever companies are producing more, investing in more machinery and materials for future production, and thus gen-

erating more jobs), employers eventually find themselves having to pay out more in wages to get a given level of goods and services produced.

Certain other factors also cause companies' labor costs to rise after business has been expanding for a time. As new, less-experienced workers are hired and must be trained, labor productivity declines. Also, knowing from past experience that the expansion will not go on forever, businesses stop introducing new machinery.

These higher wage costs per unit of output spell trouble for profits. When wage costs rise, businesses will attempt to pass on this increased cost through higher prices, taking back with one hand what they give with the other. But to the extent that they cannot raise prices, companies will decide that production is not yielding the profits they "need." So they will stop expanding production, they will not invest in new plants and machinery. Then they'll wait for reduced job security to make their employees less demanding.

Though this process affects unorganized workers as well as those belonging to unions, the results are easiest to see in statistics reflecting labor strikes. The higher the rate of unemployment, the more difficult it is for employees to stage walkouts for higher pay or better (more expensive) working conditions. Between 1972 and 1974, for instance, while the economy was expanding, the number of workers involved in strikes in the course of a year rose from 1.7 million to 2.8 million. The lifting of wage controls in April 1974 precipitated a rash of local strikes that summer, despite the absence of major contract expirations. But unemployment rates began to rise later in 1974, and the strike wave evaporated as quickly as it began. Unemployment continued to be high throughout 1975, and the number of workers involved in strikes dropped back to the 1972 level. A study of strike data from the 1950s and 1960s published in the *American Economic Review* in 1969 shows a similar pattern; the authors found that, all other factors being equal, a one-percentage-point rise in the unemployment rate cut the number of strikes by 13 percent.

The effect of unemployment on wages and the pace of work is also reflected in figures for unit labor costs — the amount employers pay in wages and fringe benefits for each unit of output (car produced, hamburger served, and so on). Unit labor costs for all private businesses rose sharply from 1972 to 1974. But between 1974 and 1976, the rate of increase *fell* from 12.5 percent to 5 percent. The effect of high unemployment in a specific industry has been clearest in recent years in the construction industry. A recent *Fortune* article on the decline of construction unions pointed out the effect of the dramatic drop in building activity during the 1974–75 recession. The business magazine noted, "When their unemployment rate soared . . . the concessions became substantial." It cited building trade pay cuts in parts of New York, Pennsylvania, and Ohio, and the willingness of "numerous unions" to enter into "project agreements" — special no-strike and cut-rate arrangements for large construction projects.

2. Overproduction. Businesses want to pay out as little as possible in wages and, at the same time, they want to somehow find customers with money to spend. Since one company's employees are another company's customers, the overall effect of holding down wages is to depress sales.

This is particularly true once a recession begins. When the auto companies, for example, slow down production, less investment goes into new machinery and equipment, hurting employment in firms that produce such industrial goods. The auto industry is also a major customer for many other industries; not only are auto workers laid off, but so too are those who work for companies supplying steel, rubber, glass, and other car parts. All these laid-off workers have to put off buying new school clothes for their kids, investing in new washers for their homes, eating out in restaurants, going to movies, or adding a garage on to their homes. So the slowdown spreads throughout the economy, and since now even fewer people can buy new cars, the auto companies lay off still more workers.

This chain reaction is analogous to a nuclear reaction — and it's about as controllable. The only solution is for the government to step in and stop it — either by buying some of the surplus goods directly, or by somehow putting spending money into people's pockets (see chapter four).

The usual term used to describe why businesses are not producing in this situation is *lack of demand.* Demanding goods because you need them, according to the logic of the profit system, is useless. The only demand to which the system reacts — technically known as *effective demand* — is one backed up by money.

3. Outlook for profits. In a general sense, recessions come about because businesses have used up their opportunities for profitable investment. Though profits make the system run, the system does not create unlimited possibilities for profitmaking. Therefore, it periodically breaks down. More specifically, a number of economic trends can cause corporate managers to decide that now is not the time to invest in equipment and materials to profitably expand production. One of these factors is inflation.

Why should businesses complain about inflation, which is just economese for rising prices? After all, they're the ones charging the new high prices. To some degree, what they're really complaining about is wages. When corporate spokespeople call for anti-inflationary policy out of Washington, the policies they have in mind are the ones that freeze wages or weaken labor by increasing unemployment. But when price increases become chronic and uncontrollable, they do pose problems for business.

The biggest problem is added difficulty in competing with lower-priced foreign goods (see chapter seven). Another, though, is the effect of inflation on corporations' ability to plan for the future.

If a company is going to invest in a new factory, a new store, or a new bowling alley that will go into operation a year from now, it wants to know what the economic situation will be when the new facility opens. Will there be demand for the

goods or services being offered? How much will it cost to run
the new operation? What kind of wages will have to be paid?
In a private, unplanned economy it's very difficult to make
these predictions. Hot-shot economists with sophisticated
computers make a lucrative business out of selling such predictions to their corporate clients, but two or more of these
predictions rarely agree. Rapid changes in prices make the
predicting even tougher. So in times of chaotic inflation, corporations are likely to be more cautious than usual about their
investment decisions.

At some point in a recession, the signs about future profitability stop saying no and start saying yes. The encouraging
signs include fewer strikes, lower interest rates, fewer surplus
goods in corporate inventories, and slower inflation. Mostly,
though, the green light is provided by government spending
or government tax cuts. Business decides that it's time to go
back to work. Production begins to increase, and recovery is
under way. But recovery for whom?

Recovery, like recession, is measured according to the
behavior of Gross National Product (or sometimes industrial
production), not the unemployment rate. There is always a
lag, in fact, between the time that production picks up and the
time unemployment shows a significant decline. After the
1958 recession, for instance, the first year of recovery saw increases of 40 percent in corporate profits and 15 percent in
industrial production, but only 2 percent in total employment.
The unemployment rate did not drop back to its prerecession
level until 1966, eight years after the slump.

A more recent example is March 1976. Recovery had
been under way for nearly a year and corporate profits were
rising again from recession levels; they were 67 percent
higher than they had been during the previous year. Yet the
unemployment rate had dropped by only one percentage
point. Joblessness was still higher than at any point since the
1930s depression; and when it would drop down to its 1973
prerecession level of 4.9 percent was — and still is — any-

body's guess. In Gary, Indiana, that March, women were picketing a steel plant that had laid off their husbands while continuing to work other employees overtime.

Manufacturing industries are the economy's leaders in showing signs of recovery; their pace of production and hiring sends the ripples through the other sectors that get them all moving again. But manufacturing companies are slow to recall their workers for two reasons. The first is that recalling full-time employees means resuming their medical insurance payments, pension fund contributions, and other fringe benefits. It's cheaper to pay overtime rates to the workers who are still employed — especially until it's clear that the recovery is going to last. The second reason is that, wherever possible, factory owners take advantage of the early stages of recovery, when their workforce is reduced and normal work relations are already disrupted, to introduce new forms of automation and speedup. Productivity figures tell the story. Output per person-hour in manufacturing, which rose only 2.7 percent in 1973 and dropped in 1974, rose by 4.9 percent in 1975 and 4.3 percent in 1976.

The Feds Step In — And Out Again

Unemployment is not going to wither away by itself. Periodic recessions are built into the structure of private, profit-oriented business decisions. By the time recoveries from these recessions come anywhere close to generating enough jobs, another recession sets in. Automation and speedup are always taking their toll and no attempt is made to use the proceeds from automation to generate new jobs.

If the normal operation of the economy can't provide jobs, can the government step in to patch things up? Can private investment decisions be influenced, or can the government put the jobless to work at public tasks? The past half-century of American economic decision making has revolved around the question of the government's role, yet full employment is as dubious a proposition as ever.

In November 1933, Franklin Roosevelt instructed Harry Hopkins, the director of the Federal Emergency Relief Administration, to put together a program of government jobs to help get the unemployed through the coming winter. This was in the depths of the depression; the spectre of widespread riots and radicalization haunted government officials. The millions of jobless were angry and disillusioned about the lack of work, the meager relief payments, and the humiliating investigations necessary to qualify for any relief at all. Hopkins' task was to quickly place several million people in federal jobs that paid a living wage.

The result was the Civil Works Administration (CWA). It was far from a guaranteed-jobs program. At its peak, it gave jobs to 4 million — about a third of the unemployed, and the bulk of the jobs were unskilled. But it reached into every county in the country and nothing like it had ever been seen before.

By January 1934, the CWA was engaged in over 400,000 different projects. CWA workers built and improved roads, airports, parks, schools, and playgrounds; they also taught in country schools and urban adult-education programs. What's more, CWA jobs paid about the same wages as were paid for equivalent work in private industry. Many CWA employees had never received these wages before.

Yet by March 31, 1934, the CWA was dead, dismantled by order of Roosevelt himself. Roosevelt had earlier announced plans to continue the program at least through May and local government officials urged that it be continued until the private economy could take over. But the administration, having successfully survived a potentially disastrous winter, now deemed the program too expensive. A major cause of the CWA's demise was opposition by private industry.

In 1934, administration aide Lincoln Colcord reported to Harry Hopkins on his talks with businessmen around the country; he summed up their opinion as one of unqualified opposition to "work relief" (as government jobs programs were then called). They objected not only because of the

cost, but because all CWA-type projects, even ditch digging, were deemed "competitive with private industry."

Winthrop Aldrich, head of the Rockefellers' Chase National Bank, announced his opposition to all forms of work relief. Liberal business leader Robert Wood, president of Sears Roebuck and a supporter of many New Deal programs, insisted that a "bare subsistence allowance" was the only permissible form of relief. An angry Southern planter wrote to Roosevelt, demanding to know how he was supposed to get plowhands at fifty cents a *day* if the government would pay them forty cents an *hour* to dig ditches.

The CWA was scuttled after four months because it competed with private industry both for work and for workers. Furthermore, it threatened to strengthen the belief of the unemployed that they had the *right* to a job. As a worried administration aide reported to the president, "They are beginning to regard the CWA as their due — that the government actually owes it to them."

Despite widespread strikes and demonstrations by CWA workers, the program was killed. It disappeared not only from the New Deal recovery effort but from the country's political memory as well. Its replacement — the Works Progress Administration (WPA) — is well known today. But the WPA, set up in 1935, paid lower wages than its predecessor, and it employed only half as many workers. The attitude of business leaders toward full employment programs was summed up by banker Frank A. Vanderlip who wrote in 1935, "I firmly believe that society does not owe every man a living."

The next federal move toward guaranteeing jobs came in 1945. World War II ended the joblessness of the depression; the unemployment rate declined an astounding fifteen percentage points between 1939 and 1944. But the expectations of victory in the war were shadowed by fears of a return to the prewar conditions in the economy. The Roosevelt and Truman administrations were under severe pressure, especially from the unions, to take some kind of action. The result was the introduction, in December 1945, of the Full Employment Act.

Sponsored by a leading liberal senator, James Murray of Montana, the bill's first draft guaranteed that all Americans willing and able to work had the right to "useful, remunerative, regular, full-time employment." It sought to guarantee "continued full employment" through the use of the federal budget.

Though attacked as "socialist" by its critics, the bill was really quite tame. It specifically stated that it did *not* authorize the government to operate any factories or other plants, and that the government had to hire private contractors for any construction work. It primarily called for federal spending at a level that would stimulate enough investment and production by private business to provide the necessary jobs.

In the event that private business did not provide the jobs, the government was to create them in public works and services in order to fill the gap. The bill specified that the budget must be a "full employment budget," and that the government's economic policies toward this goal must be "consistent" and "openly arrived at."

The bill had the strong support of the National Farmers Union (representing small farmers), the AFL, and the CIO. With administration backing, it passed the Senate with only a few modifications. (One of these, incidentally, limited the right to a job to those "seeking" work instead of "willing to work" — and limited the government's responsibility for ensuring jobs to those "who have finished their schooling and who do not have full-time housekeeping responsibilities.")

By the time the Full Employment Act reached the House, however, business was mobilized against it. The National Association of Manufacturers (NAM), in an implicit threat of a capital strike if the bill were passed, thundered that "there could be no greater discouragement to business" than this type of legislation. Donaldson Brown — a member of the Dupont family, vice president of General Motors, and director of the NAM — created a private task force to prepare testimony for the bill's opponents. (Shortly thereafter, Brown fell off a horse and broke his collarbone, so he was unable to present any of the testimony personally.)

The American Farm Bureau Federation, representing large and corporate farmers, also threw its powerful Washington lobbying apparatus against full employment. As the Southern planter had complained to Roosevelt in 1934, Farm Bureau president Ed O'Neal told the Congress in 1945 that farm owners would "resent not being able to hire help because relief projects in the community are outbidding them for labor."

The business opposition stopped the bill cold in the House. Companies needed periodic unemployment and feared giving government the power to hire the people whom they left unemployed. However, business was not unified on the question of the federal role in the economy. The view of the heads of 200 of the largest corporations, those most concerned about long-range planning, was not expressed by NAM but by the new and increasingly influential Committee for Economic Development (CED), founded in the early 1940s to plan business strategy for the postwar world.

The members of the CED had become convinced of the need for high government spending and some degree of federal management of the economy in order to guarantee continuing profits and prevent another Great Depression. The CED, the Machinery and Allied Products Institute, and other more modern business groups made suggestions toward a compromise version of the bill, which they would support. The administration agreed to go along.

So, in January of 1946, the people's representatives in Congress duly passed the "historic" Employment Act of 1946. The new law said nothing about full employment, did not put the government on record as guaranteeing the right to a job, and eliminated any direct link between the federal

budget and levels of employment. Instead, it merely directed
the government to promote the maximum employment, productivity, and purchasing power consistent with its other
goals.

Into the trash can, along with full employment, went any
real attempt to control the traditional right of business to decide when the country's economic capacity would be put to
use, and when it would not. In its place appeared a tacit commitment to use the government's spending and tax policy to
avoid politically and commercially disastrous levels of
unemployment. The new law created the Council of
Economic Advisors, the Economic Report of the President,
and the whole stable of Washington economic czars and wiz-
ards called on to predict, to cajole, and to respond to business
pressures. This setup has given us a new version of the business cycle in which the government helps call the starts and
stops (see chapter four).

The right-wing climate and relative prosperity of the 1950s
ruled out even the suggestion of anything resembling "creep-
ing socialism," but the protests of the 1960s and the hard
times of the 1970s put government job programs back on the
map.

Still, it was a question of Band-Aids, not bandwagons. The
largest of the programs — the Comprehensive Employment
and Training Act (CETA) — put a maximum of 725,000 of
the 5 to 8 million officially unemployed to work. And by official definition, CETA jobs are temporary. After a year or
eighteen months, the lucky recipient is back on the street,
knocking on the door of private industry. Last-minute congressional funding decisions, use of the jobs as political
plums, and regulations shifting money out of areas when
unemployment gets too low, all add to the insecurity.

Dissatisfaction with this type of Band-Aid during the recession of 1974–75 led to introduction, by Representative
Augustus Hawkins of California, of the Equal Opportunity
and Full Employment Act of 1975, which became known as

the Humphrey-Hawkins Bill. Its career was almost an exact replay of the 1945 bill.

The original bill — backed by women's, civil rights, and labor groups — committed the federal government to reducing unemployment to 3 percent within eighteen months of passage. It required that within four years after passage, the government would be liable to a lawsuit by any American who was left without a job. It was vague as to the means for accomplishing this, but it carried a price tag of $15 billion for job programs for the unemployed.

The bill received the expected opposition by business and was watered down to the renamed Full Employment and Balanced Growth Act of 1976. This version raised the target unemployment figure to 4 percent in four years, eliminated the right to sue, and provided only for temporary public employment programs during times of (undefined) "high unemployment." Even this version, which President Carter assured the Congressional Black Caucus was a "must piece" of legislation, was too great a departure from the American way of doing business.

Finally, in October 1978, a few hours before leaving Washington to go home and seek re-election, the Ninety-fifth Congress passed a distant cousin of the bill Hawkins had submitted three years earlier. The new law amounted to tossing pennies in a wishing well: it set a target of 4-percent unemployment in 1983, 3-percent inflation, and a reduced federal share of the economy. It also gave the president the power to declare the 4-percent unemployment level impossible to achieve. Once again, the government failed to guarantee full employment.

3.
WHAT *IS* A WOMAN'S PLACE?

Out of cattle pen tenements
where the will to live fades out
like a forty watt bulb in the hallway's crotch;
out of streets rampant with proud metal
where men are mice at work
and slavering dogs afterward;
out of beds where women offer up
their only part prized whose name
is an insult and means woman here;
where anxiety yellows the air;
where greed paints over every window;
where defeat private as a worm
gnaws every belly,
we begin our slow halting exodus.
Egypt, you formed me from your clay.
I am a doll baked in your factory ovens,
yet I have risen and walked.

— From "Exodus," by Marge Piercy,
in *The Twelve-Spoked Wheel Flashing*

In 1837, the Reverend F. Sterns, a Presbyterian minister in Newburyport, Massachusetts, stood in front of his congregation and solemnly addressed the women in his pews. "Yours it is to determine," he said, "whether the beautiful order of society shall continue as it has been," or whether "society shall break up and become a chaos of disjointed and unsightly ele-

ments." It was at home, in their "proper sphere," he continued, that women had an "almost magic power to wield the
destinies of the world." Nearly a century and half has passed
since Reverend Sterns' Sunday sermon, and it's safe to as-
sume his conclusions on women's role in the survival or down-
fall of society were somewhat overstated. Women's traditional
roles have changed, and then again, they have not. Whether
in or out of that "proper sphere," women's work is a crucial
element in today's society.

Today, as in 1837, women have the prime responsibility for
the care and maintenance of the family. Economists do not
usually recognize the existence of this work, but it is un-
ceasing and essential. Through their work in the home — by
caring and cleaning, feeding, clothing, and loving — women
help to reproduce a healthy workforce generation after generation. The family bears the responsibility for providing the
kinds of personal relations — the love, the care, the intimacy,
and the freedom of expression — that we aren't able to find
anywhere else. At the workplace, we do what we have to do;
in the marketplace, we buy what we can buy; at home, we're
supposed to be, and be respected for, ourselves. The family's
job, in an often alienating and fractured society, is to pick up
the pieces.

Sustaining the family both physically and emotionally is not
an easy task. A homemaker cleans, cooks three meals a day,
shops, organizes the family's social and leisure time, plans
and keeps the family budget, bears and rears the children.
Her responsibilities and duties are not light; as a construction
worker's wife told sociologist Anne Oakley of her work at
home: "It's as hard as doing any job . . . maybe even harder
because I'm going all the time. When my husband's job is finished, it's finished. But mine is never-ending — I mean, I get
the whole place tidy and the kids come in from school and it's
like a bomb exploded. I've no sooner done a load of laundry
and I've got another. . . . " The work of maintaining a home
and family takes long hours as well: estimates range from an

average of 99.6 hours a week (reported in a 1970 Chase Manhattan Bank study) to 44 hours per week (1975 Cleveland State Communication Research study of full-time homemakers). Whatever hours a female in the home puts in, though, doesn't alter the fact that they are all *unpaid* hours.

Women's unpaid labor for the nuclear family has serious consequences for them in and out of the home. It's a well-known characteristic in American society today that a person's value is measured in dollars and cents. Being an unpaid female homemaker brings little respect, in men's eyes, in the society's eyes, and sometimes in the eyes of women themselves. The women's movement has changed this image significantly but not completely: perceiving the duties assigned to women as being equal to those of men would require a different society with different values. Sexism and sex-defined roles keep men and women divided — a handy trait in the economic system dependent on competition rather than cooperation. Home-life roles also help to reinforce the authoritarian structures that business requires on the job. In many relations in our society, even the most intimate, there's a dominant member. Children learn early that authority rests in the hands of the parents. For married women, ultimate authority rests in the hands of the husband. In the world outside, it's the police officer or the president who's entitled to call the shots; and at work, the consciousness formed in the family allows the boss to be in control. The family, then, not only produces a workforce, but produces one accustomed to deferring to the single established authority.

Yet the family is not a static institution, and in the last century it has been affected profoundly by two interconnected economic trends. Women, including married women, are increasingly moving into paid work outside the home. And the family, once a unit within which goods were produced, has assumed more and more importance as a market for manufactured goods from outside.

These changes have revived the old outcries about the destruction of the family voiced by the good Reverend Sterns back in 1837. But they have also given rise to a new myth, that aptly dubbed by the advertising and marketing industries the "Renaissance Woman." TV ads that portray this modern wife, woman, and mother feature attractive females working in challenging, fulfilling careers. They are good mothers. They are good wives. They smell good after their hectic day of board meetings, PTA gatherings, shopping expeditions, and seven loads of laundry. They have well-adjusted families, clean kitchen floors, respectful bosses and co-workers and money in the bank. Sometimes the proud husbands of such women even proclaim, "I think I'll keep her," simply because she's so terrific. Freed from her prescribed sex role, Renaissance Woman can do it all. And do it all she does — because she has to. But not as easily or perfectly as we're made to believe.

Women in the Workplace

Women are working for wages these days in greater numbers than ever before. They are 41 percent of the workforce today. Women are venturing out of the home to find challenging careers. They are not going to work because they want the money, but because they *need* it. Many two-parent families require the income of both parents to sustain their expected standard in today's inflated economy. In 1978, the wives of 51 percent of the employed married men were also working. Wives of 57 percent of married men in the labor force, a category that also included the officially unemployed, were working — indicating that more married women go to work when their husbands are laid off. Data from 1975 show that a married woman was most likely to work a paying job if her husband made between $5,000 and $20,000 a year and least likely to work outside the home if her husband's income exceeded $25,000.

If women don't work to supplement a family income, they work to support themselves or their family alone. In 1978, 42 percent of all working women were single, widowed, di-

vorced, or separated. The number of women who shoulder
the economic responsibility for a family with no man present
reached 7.7 million in 1977, up from 5.6 million just seven
years before. That works out to nearly one out of every seven
families in the country headed by a female alone.

Entrance into the paid workforce, though, doesn't usually
mean entrance into a world without the prescribed roles of
the home. Paid work for women often consists of catering to
the public or an employer — by serving, supporting, sewing,
cooking, cleaning, recordkeeping, helping, and caring —
just as they do for their families. In 1978, the dozen leading
occupations for women were in just these roles: as secretaries, cashiers, bookkeepers, nurses, preschool and elementary school teachers; as waitresses, domestic workers,
cooks, and food-counter workers; as typists, institutional
cleaners and housekeepers, hospital aides, and sewing
machine operators. These twelve categories accounted for
41 percent of all jobs held by working women.

This work is not performed for free, as in the home, but it *is*
done for low wages. In May 1977, for instance, median incomes for two occupational groups in which women make up
the majority of workers — clerical and service work — were
$167 and $142 a week. By way of contrast, median earnings
for managers and administrators were $302 a week; for craft
workers, $259, and for machine operators, $186 per week.
There is also a good deal of inequality within general occupational groups. Within the broad job classification of clerical
workers, for instance, females make only sixty-three cents for
every dollar their male counterparts make.

Women who are able to find employment outside of the traditional sex-typed occupations and enter the job domain of
men don't fare much better. A study conducted by the National Manpower Institute's National Commission on Working
Women in 1978 found that 44 percent of the women who
held professional or managerial positions reported that they
lacked the opportunity for advancement. Their positions may
have fancy-sounding titles, but they are often dead-end,

Table 3
What Women Workers Do
(distribution by %, 1978)

Clerical workers	35
Service workers	18
Machine operators	12
Nurses and noncollege teachers	9
Other professional and technical	8
Sales	7
Managers and administrators	6
Private household workers	3
Craft workers	2
Laborers	1
Farm workers and farmers	1

Source: Compiled from Bureau of Labor Statistics, *Employment & Earnings*, January 1979. Total equals 102% due to rounding.

underpaying jobs. The same survey found that such women lacked the chance for education and training, which would enable them to get out of the dead-end positions. And one fourth of the career women questioned felt their current jobs failed to utilize their talents and skills.

The number and type of jobs that are open to women do not depend on women's abilities, but rather on employers' needs in different historical periods. In 1840, according to a contemporary occupational handbook, "few if any" females were employed as clerks in stores. Women did sewing and cleaning and they provided the cheap labor for the early textile mills. All aspects of commerce were considered men's work.

But the traditional women's occupations became overcrowded with women seeking work, providing a large pool of unemployed job seekers accustomed to relatively low wages. In the mid-1840s, New York newspapers began to editorialize in favor of women selling dry goods, so that "fine hearty lads" should not be "hived up in hot salesrooms, handing down tapes and ribbons, and cramping their genius." In the 1860s, "shopgirls" began to be hired in great numbers, possibly because so many men were away fighting the Civil War. According to a New York feminist magazine in 1868, women typically received wages half as large as those paid to male sales workers.

Likewise, office work, until the early twentieth century, was regarded as too businesslike and stressful for women. A would-be humorous engraving from 1875 depicted an office being "taken over by the ladies," who were preening before a mirror, fixing each others' hair, reading *Harper's Bazaar,* and spilling ink on the floor. In 1900, the editor of *Ladies' Home Journal* reflected on the "unnatural position of women in business." The problem "was not mental incompetence," he allowed, "but God had made her a woman and never intended her for the rougher life planned out for a man . . . it was not man that stood in her path, it was herself."

Yet at that very moment, times were changing rapidly in business. The growth of large-scale industry and the perfection of the typewriter had created a sudden demand by business for large numbers of new, low-paid employees to handle the proliferating paperwork. And nearly as sudden as these developments was the change in clerical work, which was now seen to be feminine. By 1916, another article in *Ladies' Home Journal* (by a different author), was reflecting on "the ideal stenographer," the one who could "make the most of her personal equipment." The article quoted one large employer, who expected his female help to "radiate my office with sunshine and sympathetic interest in the things I am trying to do." Between the publication dates of those two articles, the number of female office workers had quadrupled. The need for a rationale that kept women out of the office had given way to the need for one that would make them more efficient in it.

The most recent example of a dramatic change in "women's work" was female workers' entry into heavy industry during World War II. As the economy boomed after

the long depression decade and the war drew men out of the
civilian workforce, employers opened their doors to women,
who streamed into the newly available, better-paying jobs.
During one fourteen-month period, women made up 80 percent of all new workers added to factory payrolls. In many
cities, there were more women employed in factories by
1944 than there had been in the entire labor force in 1940.
At the beginning of the war, 340,000 women had been employed in heavy industry. Four years later, there were over 2
million. Corporations that until 1941 had refused to hire any
married women, or women over thirty-five, suddenly dis-
carded their rules. The proportion of women who held any
kind of paying job jumped from 29 percent in 1940 to 36
percent just four years later; it was not only new entrants to
the labor force who took advantage of the change, but many
women who had been locked into service jobs as well. A
survey by the Labor Department's Women's Bureau showed
that two thirds of the women who had worked in restaurants
and bars at the beginning of the war had transferred to other
work by the war's end. The number of black women who
worked as domestic servants fell from 72 percent to 48 percent. "Rosie the Riveter" became a national heroine. But not
for long.

Though surveys taken at the end of the war showed that
three out of four women wanted to remain on the job, it was
not to be. With men returning from the war, women were expected to leave the labor force, as insurance against a recur-
rence of the high unemployment rates of the depression.
Frederick Crawford, head of the National Association of
Manufacturers, declared that "from a humanitarian point of
view, too many women should not stay in the labor force. The
home is the basic American institution," to which women,
apparently, were expected to return willingly. Meanwhile,
under the terms of the Selective Service Act, wartime
workers were fired in order to guarantee veterans their jobs.
Layoffs in war industries sent other women packing, and
some employers reinstituted maximum age limits for women.

Detroit Edison, IBM, and other companies reimposed earlier restrictions on the hiring of married women. From 1944 to 1946, the average woman's weekly wage fell from $50 to $37.

Overall, the proportion of women in paying jobs fell back to 32 percent by 1947. In terms of steady employment for females, this decline was a serious setback, but in the long run it proved to be temporary. By the late 1950s, women's participation rate in paid work had regained its wartime peak. Throughout the decade's postwar boom, many of Rosie the Riveter's sisters and daughters managed to find new work in the lower-paying types of industrial jobs and the rapidly expanding fields of clerical work, hospital and other service work, and retail sales. By 1978, 46 percent of all women over the age of 16 were employed.

The story of Rosie the Riveter illustrates not only the arbitrariness of the divisions between "men's work" and "women's work," but also women's second-class status (shared with non-whites and teen-agers) as in-again, out-again members of the workforce. As last-hired, first-fired workers, women find it difficult to establish seniority or hold on to good jobs. Though inconvenient for women, this role as members of a reserve army of labor is quite convenient for the workings of an economic system characterized by cycles of expansion and recession. Such a system requires a pool of workers who can be mobilized during boom periods to prevent labor shortages and hold down wages and then easily dismissed during slack times.

The role of women as a reserve army is illustrated by figures on the "labor force participation" — the percentage of adult women who are working or considered to be active job seekers (see chapter two). Though the long-term trend since 1947 had been an upward one, women's participation in the labor force declined or held steady in the recessions of the 1950s and early 1970s. Just as they had in the immediate postwar years, women who in reality would have preferred to work gave up searching for hard-to-find jobs and were classified as "keeping house" rather than as unemployed members of the labor force. During the much more severe 1974–75 recession, though this phenomenon was visible in certain months, it failed to appear in the annual statistics. In other words, by that time paid work had become a more established part of women's lives and families' incomes, and they did not so easily give up actively searching for jobs. As a result, the public began to hear statements like the one made by New York bank economist Irwin Kellner in *Newsweek* in October 1976, that "the unemployment figure just doesn't mean what it used to." He blamed the large numbers of job-seeking women and teen-agers for raising the unemployment rate even though they weren't "primary breadwinners." If women would only busy themselves at home, the argument ran, unemployment would diminish.

Several other factors account for the low wages received by female workers. One is the difficulty women with children face in finding work that is compatible with their unpaid family responsibilities. It is often only the lowest-paid service occupations — such as nursing home and restaurant work — that offer any sort of part-time employment. A suburban McDonald's restaurant in which we once worked was a perfect example, relying on low-wage housewives and teen-agers to dish out the endless parade of Big Macs during peak hours. From September to June, a half dozen homemakers served up the burgers at lunchtime, arriving at 11 a.m. and leaving at 2 p.m. to meet their kids coming from school. The boss allowed them summers off as well. Dinner and summer shifts were staffed by teen-agers.

Perhaps the biggest contributor to working women's low incomes is the lack of unionization: in 1975, only 12 percent of female workers belonged to unions. Unions built a solid base in skilled crafts in the nineteenth and early twentieth centuries, and in less-skilled factory work in the 1930s and 1940s, but established unions have not made large-scale attempts to organize clerical and service workers (see chapter one). Some male unionists argue that female-dominated occupations are hard to organize because women do not take themselves seriously as workers. It is true that domestic service — which until 1940 was the leading occupation of women — is a difficult field in which to organize because both employees and employers are so dispersed. But the same is hardly true of clerical work — dominated by large banks, insurance companies, and industrial corporations — or a number of other fields.

Without serious attempts by unions to organize in these occupations, there is no factual basis for the claim that women are difficult to organize. In the textile and garment industries — which have received a lot of attention from unions — women have been active organizers and unionists since the 1840s. In clerical work today, women's groups are beginning to initiate their own union drives, affiliating with whatever established union will give them the most aid and independence.

Many unions, too, have yet to be liberated from sexism. In order to protect male members' access to scarce jobs, the AFL for many years supported legislation excluding women from such jobs as meter readers, elevator operators, and streetcar conductors as well as from night work and highly paid overtime. The massive organizing drives of the CIO doubled female union membership during the 1930s, and, during the wartime influx of women into the labor force, the CIO unions fought for the principle of equal pay for equal work. Still, there was a hitch in the efforts the CIO unions made toward organizing female employees. They established separate occupational categories and seniority lists for women, which made it easier for them to be expelled from the factories after the war.

All in all, rising participation in the labor force has brought women independent incomes, but it hasn't brought them equality with male workers on payday. In 1955, the median income for females was $2,734, putting the average woman's wage at sixty-four cents for every dollar made by the average man. Since 1950, women's labor force participation has doubled. But in 1977, the median female income was $8,814 compared to $15,070 for men — the earning power of women has declined to fifty-eight cents for every dollar earned by men.

Meanwhile, Back in the Kitchen

Parallel with women's entrance into paid work has been the growth of the family's economic importance as a market for consumer goods. Before the turn of the century, women made a lot of things used *in* the home — from bread to blankets — *at* home. But as the economy expanded, so did the search for profitable new industries and expanded markets. Home-produced goods were gradually replaced by mass-produced ones, which were built to break rather than to endure; they were not, in short, like mother used to make. Author Heidi Hartmann cites three waves in the introduction of consumer goods and services to the family between 1900 and 1930. First came the selling of utilities and services: gas, electricity, water and sewerage, garbage removal, and central heating. Second was the marketing of consumer durables like irons, vacuum cleaners, washing machines, refrigerators, and stoves. And finally came the selling of the kind of goods still flooding the market today: semi- and non-durable (goods that are used immediately or fall apart quickly) products like canned and packaged foods and ready-made clothing. Thus, over the years, families, and especially homemakers, became consumers *for* the home rather than producers *in* it.

Women are the major consumers, largely because they are responsible for making most of the family's purchases. Yet, everyone is a consumer in our society. Everyone from the oldest man to the youngest child with an allowance has to *buy* both what they need and want — the family today simply doesn't produce what it needs to live. What's more, each individual family purchases washing machines, cars, lawn mowers, and TV sets for its own use. If your lawn mower breaks down, surely your neighbors would lend you theirs. But companies don't encourage neighborhoods to buy just one mower for everyone to share — that wouldn't be good for business.

The growth of home consumption and the increase in women's participation in paid work are interdependent processes. As families need or want more mass-produced items, the need for second wage earners grows; as more and more women hold down jobs and manage homes, the need for still more labor-saving goods and services is created. And commercialization of home products and womens' more limited time in which to take care of the home have brought the commercialization of housework as well.

Just as the planning of the work process has passed from the workers who carry out the tasks to the managers and engineers who control the assembly lines, much of the power and knowledge women once held within their "proper sphere" has gone over to market researchers and product developers. Domestic hygiene, home remedies, and child-rearing techniques, once discussed and generated by groups of women, are now the profitable province of baby-soap, baby-food and child-raising how-to-books manufacturers. Women still administer the time-released cold capsule and chemically treated shampoos to the sick or slippery child, but they are administering products they know very little about.

Likewise, the preparation of fresh meats and produce has been replaced by what are now popularly referred to as convenience foods: canned peas arrived on the homefront, followed by frozen Chinese-style vegetables in a pouch; frozen TV dinners were no sooner on the table than they were outdated by freeze-dried just-add-boiling-water instant soups and lunch-box meals. And fast-food restaurants and make-it-in-a-minute microwave ovens are the glories of the convenience food trend — and are also the moneymakers for McDonald's owner Ray Kroc, and for many appliance manu-

facturers as well. The microwave oven, said one Litton Industries microwave executive, "saved the day for a lot of
appliance companies," during the rough and tumble
1974–1975 recession.

But there is some doubt whether this proliferation of
products and services has done much to increase women's
leisure time. It appears likely that household appliances, miracle cleaners, and the like, have changed the "mix" of household chores rather than lessening or eliminating them. A
woman may not have to wash, wring, hang, or fold the
laundry, but she must drag some special-fabric clothes to the
dry cleaners — plus buy and add whiteners, brighteners, and
softeners at scheduled intervals. It is undoubtedly easier to
vacuum a rug than to beat it or sweep it, but the efficiency of
the vacuum cleaner allows new, higher standards of cleanliness — new notions of what a clean rug really is. So although
it may be easier to push a vacuum cleaner than to beat a
carpet, a homemaker must devote *more* attention to a rug
more often for it to be considered clean. Specialized cleaners
for every dirt problem in the home take specialized routines
to be useful. The timesavers provided by modern business
become time*takers* instead.

A 1968 study of housework reported in the *Journal of
Home Economics* found the amount of time that modern full-
time homemakers spend on labor in the home was no less, on
the average, than the time spent in the 1920s. A similar study
conducted in 1975 showed some decline in houseworking
hours between 1965 and 1975, but it still estimated that a
total of forty-four hours were devoted to housework by unemployed women. Hours put in at home by employed
women are much lower, but the study of the National Commission on Working Women, cited earlier, found that 55 percent of the professional women surveyed and 50 percent of
clerical, sales, service, and blue-collar women said they had
no leisure time.

One burden that has not been eased by the commercialization of housework is child care. Between 1967 and 1977, the number of day-care centers in the United States grew from 10,400 to 18,300, but these centers still accommodate only 4 percent of all three- to six-year-olds with working mothers (or 7 percent of those with mothers working full-time). Centers are not only scarce, but expensive as well. "My son is not quite two years old, and I've been trying to place him in day care for several months," said a female secretary working at a Boston hospital. "If the waiting lists aren't three to six months, then the centers are too expensive. One center that had slots available was asking $14.95 per day, which adds up $74.75 a week. My take-home pay is only $111." What's more, about 60 percent of existing centers are profit-making. Commercial day-care chains are now a multimillion dollar business; the leader is Alabama-based Kinder-Care Learning Centers, Inc., with 250 centers in 23 states. Commercial centers — because they usually don't receive federal funds and so are not as strictly regulated — tend to have fewer and lower-paid staffs, and therefore less ability to provide quality care.

The most rapidly growing option is what is known as "family day care", where a woman takes care of children in her home for a fee. Because these women work for low wages, family day care is usually much less expensive — unless it's provided through an umbrella organization that adds charges for social workers, back-up services, and overhead costs. The number of family day-care units quadrupled between 1967 and 1977; the 100,000 units took in 26 percent of working mothers' three- to six-years-olds, and 36 percent of the children of women working full-time.

The remaining children — more than two thirds of the total — are cared for as they have been, in their homes or in the homes of relatives. In some instances, fathers and mothers take jobs at different times of the day or night so that someone is always at home. Equally common, the children are cared for by a grandmother, aunt, or sister. All in all, it is still often the female hand that rocks the cradle; despite women's growing place in the world of work, the duty of child care for women in the home is either unpaid or poorly paid.

The marketing of goods and services for the home brought about the growth of another industry — retailing. In the early days, those canned goods and boxes of soap were purchased at a neighboring store that carried most products a home-maker needed. But as more and more products and services arrived on the market, more and more stores sprang up to offer them space. The corner store first fell prey to the super-market; the local shopping district was transformed into today's shopping mall.

Logically enough, these changes (according to a 1968 study) added significantly more time to shopping rounds than was spent in the past. More time and energy is consumed by the task of purchasing the seemingly endless number of necessary products on the finite family budget. Shopping and budgeting, which took an average of only twenty-four min-utes a day in the 1920s, took a full hour in the late 1960s. Modern shopping malls are consciously designed to prolong this process to the utmost. Music, mirrors, waterfalls, special presentations, and displays remove shoppers from the world outside. There are rarely clocks to remind them of other duties or plans. Corners are purposely kept to a minimum in mall design, so that consumers will wander easily from one store to the next, propelled by what designers and develop-ers call "retail energy."

Buying more consumer goods, of course, means spending more. As families try to stretch their incomes like rubber bands, they fall back more and more on plastic credit cards. "Buy now, pay later" has been the watchword of the retail in-dustry since the 1950s; Master Charge, bounceable checks (checking accounts that allow consumers to overdraw on their accounts as long as they are willing to pay interest on the overdraft), and other new lending devices created by banks have swelled consumer debt even further. At the end of 1978, total outstanding consumer debt, including mortgages, reached a record $1.2 trillion — up 13 percent from a year earlier. The ratio of new consumer borrowing to net income was higher than at any time in more than a decade.

There's ample evidence that families are getting in debt way over their heads. The American Collectors Association, a collection-agency trade group, said the number of accounts turned over to collectors rose 5 percent in 1978, and the amount of money in such accounts climbed 10 percent. More than 200 credit-counseling agencies have sprung up across the country, to make a buck by advising consumers on how to break their addiction to borrowing. Personal bankruptcies, after three years of decline, were also on the upswing. Resorting to bankruptcy is the most extreme measure, but anyone who has overextended his or her credit line can understand why one retired truck driver in Boston filed last spring: "I had gotten into a bind, and I couldn't see the way out. I didn't have two nickels to rub together." The falling incomes that come with a recession could bring still more families into bankruptcy court.

Reverend Sterns and the New Right

The economic changes surrounding the traditional nuclear family *have* been substantial: the growing economic dependence of women, their likelihood of working a double shift at home and at a job, the exaltation of consumption as the goal of the family. It appears, in fact, the institution has taken quite a beating. Family tensions are absent from the life of the "Renaissance Woman" in TV commercials, but the divorce statistics tell another story. In 1935, of all thirty-year-old women who had ever been married, fewer than 6 percent had seen their first marriage end in divorce. By 1975, nearly 17 percent of thirty-year-old females were divorced at least once. In recent decades, women are marrying later and living outside of marriages more. Between 1960 and 1978, the proportion of women between the ages of eighteen and sixty-four who had never married rose from 13 percent to 18 percent. The proportion who were separated or divorced and had not remarried rose from 6 percent to 11 percent. And the proportion living in the traditional family — married with husband present — dropped from 73 percent to 64 percent.

Divorce, later marriage, no marriage at all. Have Reverend Sterns' long-ago predictions indeed come true? Has the "beautiful order of society" turned into that chaos of "disjointed and unsightly elements" he feared?

That's the way the new political Right tells it: the family, its spokespeople say, has begun to crumble; women have a duty to hold it steadfast against the turning tides of time. Anita Bryant blames homosexuality, Congressman Henry Hyde professes abortions are weakening our home lives, Phyllis Schlafly points at the Equal Rights Amendment, Marabel Morgan claims that female independence has ruined the Total Woman. Their pitch usually combines a little modern-day psychology with some old-time religion. Morgan's Total Woman, for instance, can "cater to her man's special quirks, whether it be in salads, sex or sports." But Morgan makes sure a Total Woman remembers who is in control: "It is only through God's power that we can love and accept others, including our husbands. It is only when a woman surrenders her life to her husband, reveres and worships him, and is willing to serve him, that she becomes really beautiful to him."

Likewise, a late-1970s John Birch Society pamphlet exalts the roles of the submissive and faithful wife and mother.

Traditionally a man's role as head of the family takes him away from the hearthstone. A woman is like many stones: she is decorative, exotic stones hedging and protecting precious and beautiful growth; she is graceful as marble, preserving culture and tradition; and she is hard as granite with anything that threatens her home and her children. She is soapstone and pumice, ever-cleansing and smoothing; she is touchstone; a close comfort to her mate and little ones. And she sometimes feels like a well-worn cobblestone over which have passed the tribulations of all she holds dear. . . . She can

be ruby-lipped, onyx-eyed, pearl-skinned and topaz-tressed.
But always she shines like the symbol of her marriage, the
perfect diamond that will reflect her growth from bride to
grandmother.

Onyx-eyed and topaz-tressed. It's a pitch out of another
century, but a lot of political mileage can be gained from
harking back to the good old days, whether or not they ever
really existed. If Henry Hyde and Howard Jarvis could win
their crusades, there's some chance that Phyllis Schlafly and
friends can do the same. Yet the economic reality is that there
is no going back, so sooner or later we are going to have to
go forward. That means finding ways for society to shoulder
some of the responsibility for raising children and allowing
individual expression — functions that women and the family
are still wholly responsible for. It means too that new, non-
sexist attitudes must be developed both at home and at work,
so that men and women can equally share in the financial support and the chores of maintaining the home and family.

4.
GOVERNMENT: BIG AND GETTING BIGGER

*I don't think anyone really comes to work in the govern-
ment thinking they're going to see a lot get done. I know I
didn't. But people come with a kind of classic liberal ideal
about ameliorating the plight of the poor and restraining
the growth of inequality — and they believe that by their
presence, because they're willing to work harder and more
steadfastly than the people before them, they're going to
make government better. Ten years down the road, they
turn into the people that the next wave will have the same
feelings about.*

*There's a basic rule of thumb that people quote here:
that Congress is reactive rather than active. To promote
any kind of progressive program that's not in response to
popular pressure — that would be urging the Congress to
step into unchartered waters where there's no knowing
what the repercussions will be. Congress doesn't want to
do that.*

*I remember that back in 1968 when I was in college, we
forced the faculty senate to vote against Defense Department research on our campus; six months later they re-
scinded the vote when everyone was away for vacation.
Congress is very much like that bunch of guys. If the heat's
on them, then they'll do something; a surly crowd outside
conjures up the kind of images that get Congress to act.
Once that heat's gone they'll go back to the passive role
they're comfortable with.*

The second thing to keep in mind is that Congress's fundamental concern is prosperity. That's what Congresspeople think gets them elected. Now when they consider programs that redistribute income or change the way economic institutions work, they inevitably run up against someone who tells them that they're jeopardizing prosperity. Somehow the nation's largest corporations — who speak to Congress through their own representatives and trade and industry association people — will come around in the face of anything and say, 'You're jeopardizing prosperity.' The impression you get is that prosperity is a person who they've kidnapped and locked away in a closet, Patty Hearst style. And like a grade-B movie, they tell you, 'You leave me no choice.' If you mess with them, they're gonna cut prosperity's toe off and nail it to you.

The big example recently has been oil price deregulation. What you hear is, 'Unless you let us have those bucks, then we're not going to be able to produce new oil.' Two years ago, when Congress was considering strengthening the minimum wage law, we were inundated with letters from fast-food joints saying that that was the kiss of death for the quickie hamburger. The argument is always the same: 'We're the only people that can carry prosperity on for you, and if you fuck with us, you're fucking with the thing that we have in our hands for you.'

It's always been my impression that the federal government didn't start running the country until about 1910. I mean, if you look at the private armies that were held by the magnates and tycoons in the late 1800s — the Harrimans had a private army of 50,000 men that cleared the tracks for them and so forth. The government used to hire Pinkertons to do some of its work because they were tougher than the government was. The government only got bigger than those guys around 1910. And it's still not really bigger, you know? People resent paying taxes, and they're probably entitled to some extent to feel that they're

being impoverished by a government they don't under-
stand and can't see as being in their interest. But the gov-
ernment doesn't have the clout to stand up to a lot of pri-
vate sector actors and trends; it's really powerless unless it
decided to break its own rules. Especially with the growth
and transnationalization of the largest corporations, the
government is really just the tail on a horrifyingly central-
ized dog. What can it do but follow the rest of the beast?"

—U.S. Congressional staff member,
Washington, D.C., May 1979

Visit Washington, D.C., and you'll find yourself strangely
insulated from the rhythm of economic life. No steel mills
belch smoke into the sky, no banks or insurance companies
scrape the skyline with glassy monuments to themselves;
you'll see no stockyards, no refineries, no port. Yet the
capital, increasingly, is the center of attention, the focus of
economic demands and debate.

Will Washington bail out New York City? Will Congress
balance the budget? Will the president's policies bring inflation or recession? Will national health insurance free us from
runaway medical costs or bankrupt the government? Should
Washington control oil prices, oil companies; limit imports;
regulate wages; shorten the work week; raise or lower interest rates? On a smaller scale, the same attention centers on
state capitals and city halls across the country. Big government and bureaucracy are fast becoming the official national
scapegoats, yet the fact is, they have also become an insepa-
rable part of our economic system.

Why Big Government?

The most striking sign of the governmental role in the economy is how much the public treasuries spend. Between 1929
and 1978, spending by all levels of government increased
from one tenth to one third of the Gross National Product. In

1978, that total was $684 billion. About 56 percent of the total was direct federal government spending; 11 percent was federal grants to states and localities; money raised and spent by state and local governments accounted for the remaining 33 percent. Much of the federal outlay goes to payroll; government has also become a major employer. State and local officials now sign the paychecks of 13 percent of all employed people in the country. The federal government's civilian employees account for another 3 percent; the armed forces, 2 percent more.

The purposes of government spending vary widely, but they can be summed up in two major categories. First, governments spend in response to the demands of private business for subsidization and stimulation. Second, they spend in response to demands of popular movements for solutions to the problems that the private sector economy creates but cannot handle.

Corporations need many particular government programs in order to create the basis for profitable operations. In some cases the government actually absorbs the costs of private business; examples range from research and development funding and investment tax credits to industrial park construction. In others, it provides services that make private business possible. Highway construction, for instance, gave an essential push to the auto, oil, trucking, and related industries. Military intelligence, aid, and protection are extended to foreign governments that offer an open door to U.S. business; U.S. armed forces are maintained in readiness for interventions like those in Vietnam and the Dominican Republic when nationalist or socialist regimes threaten to take power.

These are examples of subsidization. But aside from the question of *what* the money is spent on, business requires a certain *amount* of government spending to stimulate the economy — to guarantee a sufficient level of sales of its products and services. Despite the official commitment of most presidential administrations to a balanced budget, the federal government has overspent in forty-two of the fifty fis-

cal years since the onset of the Great Depression. Left to its
own devices, business simply will not invest enough money in
new equipment or pay out enough in wages to the workers
who are the bulk of the nation's consumers to keep the
economy running. The need for business stimulation has been
an underlying cause of the steady increase in public spending
over the past half century.

Government spending on military and highway programs
were the fastest growing spending categories in the 1950s.
But after 1960, despite the rise in military spending during
the Vietnam War, there was a pronounced overall shift toward social services and aid to individuals. In part, this
change was a response to the explosion of protest and community organization unleashed by the struggles of the civil
rights movement. The root causes of poverty, economic insecurity, decaying cities, and a deteriorating environment were
not eliminated, but governments were forced to step in with a
wide variety of programs to alleviate the most serious crises
— programs that ranged from rent supplements to health
clinics to open city college enrollment. Also, the cost of
providing services rose, as the 1960s and 1970s saw a significant growth in unionization among public employees.
Teachers, too, sang "We Shall Overcome" as they sought on-
the-job protection from too much work for too little pay.

Still, even in the area of social services, government programs contain elements that are designed to reduce corporate costs. Education spending — which grew from 13 percent
to 18 percent of all government expenditures during the
1960s — most directly merges the needs of business with demands for reform. Seen by most people as a route to better-
paying and more secure jobs, public education also offers
business extensive free training and disciplining of future
workers. The growth of public aid to higher education in the
1960s in part reflected the needs of increasingly technological and bureaucratized industries.

Health programs also play this dual role. Medicare and
Medicaid respond to the needs and demands of the elderly

and poor. But their function is not so much to supply quality health care as to ensure that the bills of private drug companies, doctors, and hospitals will be paid. Medicare, which is funded by the social security tax, is simply a mandatory payroll deduction for old-age insurance; it has helped to create a highly profitable nursing home industry, but not a high-quality one. Thus the form of government spending — even on services that are responses to popular need and pressure — is often distorted by the needs of business.

Trouble in Paradise

Although the government has attempted to use its spending power to stave off economic and social crises, it has not entirely succeeded in doing so. It has, however, altered the forms of crisis. It has displaced some of the problems faced by business, and some of the problems caused by business, from the private sector of the economy to the public sector. Now, as the weaknesses of the economy become more and more evident, government spending is being attacked as the *cause* of a crisis of which it is really only a *symptom*. Especially, the gains of the political struggles of the 1960s have been singled out as the sacrificial lambs.

The first wave of trouble was the urban fiscal crisis — the public sector by-product of the deep recession that hit the economy in 1974. Many cities were already in vulnerable positions because of the departure of industry and more affluent residents. Publicly funded highway networks reaching out into suburbs and less-developed regions were a further incentive for companies to leave cities for greener pastures. City governments were left with the task of maintaining services for increasingly poor, deteriorating, jobless, and crime-ridden neighborhoods. Increases in health, police, educational, and other programs led to a 72 percent jump in nationwide municipal employment between 1960 and 1973.

In the recession, sales and incomes fell, and tax revenues fell along with them. At the same time, with more people out of work, the need for city services was, if anything, greater. Thus cities and some states — especially in the older manufacturing regions of the Northeast and Midwest — had to borrow more and more funds in order to pay their bills. In 1975, New York City was spending one sixth of its budget to pay off its debts.

The fiscal crisis was bad news in city hall, but it was good news in the board rooms of the major banks. When cities borrow, they do it by issuing short-term interest-bearing notes or longer-term interest-bearing bonds. In either case, the cities don't do the marketing directly, they do it through underwriters — banks and stock brokers — who buy some of the bonds and notes themselves and sell the rest to other investors. Underwriters collect lucrative commissions for their services, but, more important, they gain the power to "suggest" what levels of interest must be paid in order to make the notes and bonds marketable. When the banks lost confidence in New York City in the summer of 1974, they amazed city officials by demanding an interest rate of 7.9 percent — outrageous by past standards. A year later they were getting 11 percent.

Still more important, though, is the political power that such a fiscal crisis gives the banks. In many cities and some states, bankers have been able to dictate the cuts governments have to make if they want to continue to get loans. In New York — the most extreme example — control of the city budget actually passed out of the hands of locally elected officials and into those of the Municipal Assistance Corporation and the Emergency Financial Control Board, both dominated by corporate executives. But across the country, officially or unofficially, the message was the same — freeze wages, cut pensions if possible, eliminate services, lay off municipal workers. City employees and city residents were to bear the brunt of the economic crisis in order to ensure the safe collection of the banks' loans.

New York laid off 60,000 people in two and a half years. Boston reduced its payroll by more than 10 percent. Birming-

ham, Detroit, Milwaukee, Seattle, and St. Louis were among
other major cities that cut jobs significantly. Taking the United
States as a whole, the number of municipal workers dropped
by 1.7 percent in 1976 — the first decline in fifteen years. Between October 1973 and October 1976 prices rose 27 percent, but average wages for city workers rose only 20
percent. And sure enough, surpluses began to replace
deficits on municipal balance sheets.

When cities cut back their workforces, the level and quality
of services falls as well. Public hospitals close or get more
crowded, parks deteriorate, school classes get larger and
special programs are dropped, garbage stays on the streets,
day-care centers are closed, fire fighters and police take
longer to answer calls, and all the while the fiscal health of
cities continues to improve. In the satisfied words of the *Wall
Street Journal,* since the advent of the fiscal crisis "many cities
aren't attempting to address social ills which they might have
felt compelled to attack five or ten years ago."

The visible villians in the fiscal crisis are the bankers, but in
this case as in others the bankers are acting as representatives
of business as a whole. Behind Citibank's and Chase Manhattan's "solution" to the crisis of the mid-1970s lay often-
voiced corporate concern with "capital formation." As we've
said, certain levels and types of government spending are
necessary to create the conditions for profitable corporate
operations. But too great a share of the nation's resources
going into government social services does not contribute to
the amassing of private capital. There is only so much to go
around, and business felt it was not getting a satisfactory
share. Too much borrowing by the various levels of government, for instance, meant higher interest rates and a scarcity
of borrowable funds for corporations; government was said
to be "crowding out" private business in the "capital markets."
Likewise, high government spending contributed to higher
corporate taxes. The business community wanted this situation reversed by the time economic recovery rolled around.

As Chase Manhattan informed the American public in a

series of newspaper ads in the spring of 1975, "Capital formation must be the government's business, business's business, labor's business, banking's business — everybody's business." A *Business Week* editor writing the previous fall had been blunter: "Indeed, cities and states, the home mortgage market, small business, and the consumer, will all get less than they want because the basic health of the U.S. is based on the basic health of its corporations and banks." But something more persuasive than public relations campaigns was needed to get that message across. The fiscal dilemma of the cities — pushed just short of bankruptcy by the financial institutions' unwillingness to lend — was just the ticket.

The fiscal crisis had a major drawback, though. Effective as it was, it focused an unprecedented amount of public anger on the banks. "The banks are bastards and First National City Bank is the biggest bastard," declaimed a New York city councilor in March 1975. "The bankers are robbing the city with interest rates. [First National City Bank chairman] Wriston wants us to fire cops and school teachers, and close up daycare centers and firehouses, so he can make more profits." The most recent use of the fiscal crisis gambit — by Cleveland banks trying to force the city to sell its municipal electric company to a private monopoly firm — was successfully blocked by the city's mayor via a public referendum. It may be for this reason that the current round of attacks on public services and public employees has come in a more populist guise — the tax revolt. But today's tax revolt is essentially a replay of the fiscal crisis, with a focus on state and federal budgets and on the political arena.

There is some real basis for public anger over taxes. Because of the government's growing role in the economy, between 1957 and 1977 taxes gradually rose from 25 percent to 30 percent of the Gross National Product. It's hard to come up with a figure showing the change in an average individual's tax burden, but comparing total taxes to total income shows a similar increased bite of about 5 percent over the two decades. So people are spending somewhat more of their incomes on "buying" government than they used to. At the same time, the level of confidence in government has steadily decreased as a result of the Vietnam War, Watergate, the faltering economy, and the failure of liberal social programs to really solve social problems.

Perhaps most important, rising taxes are the only form of inflation that people have the power to vote against. Again, as the government has taken over the function of feeding and cleaning up after private business, it has become the target for public anger that would be better directed at business itself. In the 1950s and 1960s when incomes were rising, most people did little more than grumble over the increasing tax bite; next year's income would be higher in any case. Now, however, even relatively well paid workers are unable to make much headway against inflation, and many are threatened by unemployment as well. There is not much left to pay the tax collector.

A similar logic applies to business. Faced with inflation and with uncertainty about future sales, corporations have become especially interested in cutting costs. Taxes are a cost to be cut. Corporations do not want all of government's functions in the economy limited, but they believe this is a safe time to roll back some services won by grass-roots struggles in the 1960s and to tighten up on payrolls and working conditions in the public sector. These actions increase companies' bargaining power with their own employees as well. Limiting the growth of taxes and spending, from the point of view of business, can lessen both the squeeze on profits and the popular discontent over high taxes, while forcing public employees, the poor, community groups, and some special business interests to fight among themselves for whatever funds are available.

The leadership of the tax revolt is usually associated with Howard Jarvis, the California real-estate millionaire who masterminded the property tax–slashing Proposition 13. But national and multinational corporations — represented by an organization called the National Tax Limitation Committee

(NTLC) — have been pushing somewhat more moderate programs in more than thirty states. In Michigan, for instance, an NTLC affiliate called Michigan Taxpayers United is backed by such major corporations as Ford and Dow Chemical. In November 1978, it won voter approval of a measure to limit state spending to its present proportion of total personal income.

On the national level, the same forces are at work. One extreme proposal would require a balanced budget every year, while another demands a one-third slash in federal spending. But the NTLC has put forward an alternative proposal — whose drafters include conservative economist Milton Friedman and Ford Motor Company chief economist William Niskanen — to link spending levels to the overall growth of the economy and the rate of inflation. Their plan would also permit Congress to exceed this ceiling with a two-thirds vote, ensuring greater flexibility in the event of wars or serious recessions but effectively holding the line against any social service or full-employment programs that business wants to block.

Either way, the emphasis on limiting the *total* tax bill serves to distract attention from the particular way in which tax and spending limits are being applied. That is, *whose* taxes are being cut, and *what* government programs are being sacrificed. We've already discussed the content of the spending cutbacks at the local level and we'll have more to say about the federal level later in the chapter when we discuss the attempt to restore the dominance of military spending. For now, let's take a look at the question that is always carefully avoided by the spokespeople for the tax revolt — who pays the taxes?

The most recent major study of the distribution of the tax burden was published in 1974 by the Brookings Institution, a big Washington think tank. The authors of the study devised several difference procedures to calculate how all the different taxes — local, state, and federal — hit different income groups. According to one of their major calculations, all families end up paying one quarter of their income in taxes, regardless of their income level! That is, if you take all levels of taxes, and calculate what people actually pay after all deductions and hidden taxes are accounted for, everyone ends up in the same tax bracket, from the highest to the lowest paid.

(Another calculation used in the study — the one most lenient toward the present setup — did not recognize that any property taxes are passed on to tenants or that any corporation taxes are passed on to consumers. Still, even according to this calculation, most people pay about 23 percent of their income in taxes, while the poorest fifth of the population pays 18 percent and the richest fifth pays 27 percent.)

The Brookings study found that federal taxes are slightly progressive — that is, they end up taxing richer people at a slightly higher percentage of their income. But they are balanced by state and local taxes, which are tilted the other way. Recent changes in tax laws in the climate of the tax revolt have done nothing to improve this situation. If anything, they've made it worse. California's Proposition 13 brought windfalls to large apartment owners, but nothing to tenants. The news from the federal level is no better, despite the Carter Administration's promised tax reform.

In the third week of the 1976 presidential election campaign, candidate Carter insisted, "We will shift the burden of taxes to where the Republicans have always protected — on the rich, the big corporations, and the special interest groups — and you can depend on that if I am elected." What President Carter actually sent to Congress, in 1978, was a tax package that would cut just $250 to $325 from the federal income tax bill of a four-person family, whether that family made $10,000 a year or $100,000. For corporations, he proposed to close some loopholes while widening others and reducing the tax rate — yielding a total corporate tax cut of more than $5 billion.

By the time the proposal got through Congress, even the minor reforms had been eliminated. In their place appeared a new handout to the rich: a $2.2 billion easing of the tax on capital gains. *Capital gains* is the name given by the tax code to income from selling stocks, real estate, and other assets that have increased in value since they were purchased. Some of these gains are not taxed at all, and the rest are taxed at a lower rate than other income. In 1974, people earning between $10,000 and $15,000 a year saved an average of $19 on their tax bills through the use of this loophole; those making over $100,000 saved an average of $19,000! Thanks to Congress's enthusiasm for "cutting taxes," upper-income taxpayers will now save even more. As one corporate tax specialist told *Business Week* when Congress had completed its work, "It's a relief to look at a tax bill and not have it called 'tax reform.'"

The Political Business Cycle

There is another drama underlying tax and spending policy — especially at the federal level — which must be understood if the whole pageant of economic decision-making in the government is to make sense. Setting the overall level of taxes and spending is the heart of what is known as fiscal policy, which is in turn a key aspect of the federal government's attempt to manage the business cycle described in chapter two. Fiscal policy is the use of the government's spending and taxing powers to affect the levels of employment, production, and prices in the national economy.

The more the government spends — or the less it taxes — the more money it is pumping into the economy. Either the government is paying individuals (government workers, unemployment compensation, or welfare recipients) who will spend the money for what they need, or it is paying contractors (to build airplanes, do medical research, or supply computers to federal agencies), or it is encouraging business and consumer spending through tax cuts or rebates. The less the government spends — or the more it taxes — the less demand there is for the goods and services that businesses have for sale.

The simplest figure to look at to see whether the government is carrying out a policy of stimulating the economy or one of slowing it down is the budget deficit — the amount by which spending exceeds taxes. The higher the deficit, the more the economy will be stimulated: more products will be sold and more people will have jobs. The lower the deficit, the lower the overall demand for goods and services and the more the economy will move toward recession.

(Besides fiscal policy, the government also makes use of monetary policy to speed up or slow down the economy. The details are murky, but the essence is manipulating interest rates and the availability of bank loans through actions by the system of twelve Federal Reserve Banks. *Loose money* — low interest and easy credit — encourages private spending and stimulates the economy whereas *tight money* — high interest and hard-to-get loans — puts on the brakes.)

Sounds pretty simple, right? Keep running deficits, and avoid recessions. One problem with this panacea is that it results in the steady build-up of the public debt. The more basic problem, however, is that the operation of an economy based on private profit *requires* recessions.

The major reasons for recessions were discussed in chapter two. When the economy runs too close to full employment for too long, workers' wage increases tend to speed up and their productivity increases tend to slow down; the profit picture begins to darken. Also, when there are sustained high levels of purchases of goods and services, businesses have the opportunity to raise prices at will; the resulting inflation, however, poses a threat to their ability to plan and to compete internationally. So, eventually, companies become cautious about increasing production, setting off a chain reaction of layoffs, lower sales, more layoffs . . . and the recession is on.

The purpose of government fiscal policy is not to end this cycle, which is rooted in the form of organization of the private sector. Rather, the purpose is to manage it. When recessions get too deep, the government increases spending or cuts taxes in order to push the economy toward recovery. When the recovery has gone on too long, taxes are raised or spending is cut.

The federal government has never pursued a policy of continuous stimulation, because sooner or later business demands an end to it. In late May of 1978, for instance, *Business Week* featured a lead editorial entitled "If a Recession Starts." The magazine praised the administration and Congress for holding down spending and tightening monetary policy, but it warned that "the big test of nerve still lies ahead. It will come when the long upswing in the economy loses momentum and the nation goes into a new recession. That time may well be in the near future.... Congress should determine now to stick by its commitment to a tight budget and let the economy set its own pace."

The speed with which this message gets to the White House is in part a reflection of politicians' dependence on corporate dollars for their campaign chests and corporate experts to make their policies. When Jimmy Carter arrived in the White House, for instance, he chose the heads of giant corporations for two key economic posts. W. Michael Blumenthal, secretary of the treasury, came to Washington after having led the Bendix Corporation to the seventieth position on *Fortune* magazine's roster of the 500 largest U.S.-based manufacturers. The *Wall Street Journal* strongly endorsed Blumenthal's selection, noting that he is "known as a business-world liberal, which is fine; business-world liberals understand the role and needs of business." For chairman of the Federal Reserve Board, the administration turned to G. William Miller, who had presided over a Rhode Island–based conglomerate called Textron. Miller's seventeen-year guidance over the company's growth led it to the eighty-third spot on *Fortune*'s list by the year of his appointment to the Federal Reserve Board.

But the politicians' cozy relations with corporate executives are only the pale reflection of a more frightening reality. Even

the most populist of politicians would have to accede to corporate pressures for recession eventually, unless he or she
was willing and able to begin changing economic funda-
mentals. As long as the corporations own and control society's productive capacity, they are the ones holding all the
cards. Workers are not the only ones who can strike when the
income outlook is bad; business goes on strike as well. But it's
not labor that business holds back, it's investment capital.
They can and do refuse to invest in new machinery to expand
or even maintain production. This is most obvious when it
happens in a specific industry, like oil or natural gas (see
chapter five), but in a general way, it is what happens in all recessions. Although corporate chieftains are known to meet
frequently in lobbying and policy-formation groups to prepare their recommendations for economic policy, this
scenario does not require a conspiracy; it merely requires the
making of sound business decisions about the timing of profitable investments.

In theory, the same thing is true of ending recessions. Eventually, high unemployment should result in smaller wage demands, higher productivity, and less inflation; businesses
should begin making new investments and rehiring workers
on their own. In practice, ever since the Great Depression
economic slumps have always been ended with the help of
government action. The reasons why the economy does not
"self-correct" are many and varied, relating both to technical
problems such as the build-up of corporate debt and to long-
run problems of the system's inability to generate enough
profitable investment opportunities. Perhaps a deep enough
depression would eventually correct itself, but since the
1930s politicians and capitalists have justifiably feared the
radicalization such a depression would bring about.

A particular difficulty that has appeared in recent recessions is the failure of inflation to slow down despite increasing
unemployment. This unexpected phenomenon is known in
economists' jargon as *stagflation*. Between January 1974 and
January 1975, as the official unemployment rate soared from

5.2 percent to 8.2 percent, the annual rate of inflation also rose sharply — from 9.4 percent to 11.2 percent. It took still another year of high unemployment to get the annual rate of price increases down to even as low as 7 percent. Finally, in 1976, inflation slowed to a rate of 5 percent — and then began to speed up again as the economy gained steam.

In theory, as more people are thrown out of work and their purchasing power falls, companies should begin to lower prices in an effort to boost sagging sales. One reason they don't do so is the growth of monopoly (to be discussed in the next chapter). Another reason, paradoxically enough, is the growth of the government's role. Because corporations expect the government to step in sooner or later, they are more prepared to ride out the recession without cutting their prices. Whatever the cause, the recent history of the economy shows that it takes deeper and deeper recessions to create even temporary slowdowns in inflation.

Yet more and more, recessionary policies are justified in the name of fighting inflation. The president, after all, cannot go on TV and announce that 3 million people are going to be laid off in order to keep up profits, productivity, and U.S. corporations' ability to compete with German corporations. So budget cuts or higher interest rates are presented as everyone's weapons in the war against Public Enemy Number One — inflation. But the fact is that there are different means of responding to inflation that would benefit different groups in society.

Wage increases — and particularly full cost-of-living clauses in contracts — would be much more beneficial to most Americans than recessions. So would strict price controls. These forms of protection would not be easy to win, since they too run up against the power of corporations to go on strike. But depending on the government to "Whip Inflation Now" through spending cuts and tight money is a false and potentially disastrous hope. Government economists will continue to predict that they can produce stable rates of unemployment and inflation, satisfactory to all. But the pat-

tern of the last decade doesn't speak well for their ability to
fine tune the economy.

Billions for Bombers

No discussion of the government's role in the economy is
complete without an examination of the largest area of federal spending — one that recent administrations have tried to
exempt from their new-found fiscal responsibility — the military budget.

The continuation of wartime levels of military outlays in the
1950s in the newly invented situation of the Cold War
provided the rationale for the new policy of government
spending to stimulate the economy. In that decade, outlays
for national defense accounted for over 50 percent of federal
government spending. (This calculation — like others that will
follow — does not include additional military costs such as interest payments left over from past wars, veterans' benefits,
or military retirement pay.)

Beefing up the armed forces was then and is today business's favorite form of government spending. Multinational
corporations need the U.S. military to act as a global police-
man, and bases stretch from Puerto Rico to the Philippines;
but there are also domestic economic aspects of weapons
expenditures that make them, from a corporate point of view,
unique.

Quite simply put, when the government buys weapons it
does not compete with private corporations. If the government was to get serious about building housing or setting up a
national health system, it would be in direct competition with
building contractors, real-estate developers, landlords,
doctors, and hospitals. If the government was to put sizable
amounts of money into high-quality subsidized mass transit,
where would that leave Ford and GM? When the government makes noises about hiring too many of the unemployed,
as we've already seen, business leaders suddenly cry foul.

But if Washington wants to pay private corporations to

build some bombers or nuclear submarines — things these private companies would otherwise have almost no market for — who's going to kick? Not General Motors, General Electric, General Dynamics, or any of the civilian Generals firmly ensconced on the Pentagon payroll. No government program except the race to space offers so many advantages and so few drawbacks. A certain unpleasant connection with foreign wars and nuclear holocaust is not considered a serious liability.

The popular argument for a big military budget — aside from the Chinese, Russian, or other appropriate communist threat — is that it is supposed to provide jobs. The fact is that any other type of spending would provide at least as many jobs, and probably more. Military spending is weighted toward high-technology products that require fewer workers than other products or services. The federal Bureau of Labor Statistics found in 1975 that $1 billion in defense spending produced 74,000 jobs; the same amount spent through the National Institutes of Health yielded 84,000 jobs, whereas $1 billion put into occupational training and public job programs employed 136,000. Another study, by the Michigan branch of the Public Interest Research Group (PIRG), found that federal aid to states and localities was worth 100,000 jobs per billion dollars. Overall, the Michigan group found that taking $1 billion from the military and spreading it instead over the civilian economy — private as well as public — would create an additional 10,000 jobs.

In the early 1960s, as other types of federal spending grew, the Pentagon's share of the federal budget dropped sharply — from 50 percent in 1959 to 40 percent in 1965. Then the Vietnam War reversed the trend. Despite the increase in spending on the War on Poverty and other domestic programs, the military share of the budget bounced back up to 44 percent by 1968. The Johnson Administration, trying to salvage an increasingly unpopular war by promising to deliver both "guns and butter," ran into serious economic difficulties as a result. Though unemployment was low and the economy was not really in need of stimulation, the administration had to run large deficits to finance the war. As early as 1966, David Rockefeller went on record urging an income tax increase. But a tax to pay for Vietnam was politically impossible; the surcharge finally enacted in 1968 was too little too late. The extent to which the economy was overstimulated in this period helps account for the severity of the recession "needed" to slow it down in the 1970s.

Because of the antimilitary climate created by the war, the Pentagon had trouble maintaining its share of the budget after the beginning of de-escalation. Though the dollar amount spent on the military has increased in most years since 1968, "real military spending" (that is, corrected for inflation) declined steadily through 1976. At the same time, spending on social security, health, public assistance, and job programs has increased rapidly as a result of demographic changes, soaring health care costs, and recession. Therefore the share of the budget spent on the military has dropped to 23 percent by fiscal year 1979.

In the last few years, however, presidential administrations have been trying to turn this trend around. Gerald Ford's attempts to win an increase in real military outlays were defeated by the Democratic Congress. With Carter in the White House, things have gone more smoothly. Between 1976 and 1979, real military spending rose an average of 1.4 percent a year. The budget Carter presented for fiscal 1980 — despite cuts in many programs — included a projected after-inflation hike of 3.1 percent for the Pentagon. It also projected devoting an increased share of the total budget to the military for the first time in twelve years.

Nevertheless, there have been some victories in pruning the military budget in recent years — most notably the successful four-year campaign by a grass-roots national coalition to stop the proposed fleet of 244 B-1 bombers priced at $110 million apiece. But there has also been a growing sophistication on the part of some military-spending advocates about avoiding such obvious boondoggles. By 1977, former secre-

Table 4
Where Your Federal Tax Dollar Goes (by %)

Defense	23.2
Social security	20.1
Interest on debt	10.7
Health	10.0
Public assistance and services	6.9
Government employee retirement	4.2
Veterans' benefits and services	4.1
Transportation	3.5
Unemployment compensation	3.2
Education	2.5
Employment and training	2.5
Other, smaller categories	9.1

Source: Compiled from estimated outlays for fiscal year 1978, *The U.S. Budget in Brief, Fiscal Year 1979.*

Note: The percentage of your *income tax* dollar going to military spending or interest payments is significantly higher, since social security, Medicare, and several other programs are paid for out of special trust funds financed by separate taxes.

tary of defense (and corporate lawyer and director) Clark Clifford and Vietnam War architect McGeorge Bundy had added their voices to the anti–B-1 chorus. A study by the Brookings Institution likewise urged the abandonment of such "needlessly expensive weapons" in order to create a "new consensus" around overall high military spending.

Despite all the ups and downs, the military budget continues to be the largest single element in the federal budget, and it will likewise continue to be surrounded by controversy. The attempt by business and government to revive military spending at a time when government services and public employees are bearing the brunt of economic crisis is another sign that there's more to the question of big government than meets the eye.

5.
MONOPOLY: MORE THAN A GAME

Charles B. Darrow was born in the opening year of the twentieth century. By the time he reached the age of twenty-nine, he was a prosperous heating engineer residing in the Philadelphia suburb of Germantown. The depression arrived and Darrow's job and his money departed. He took to repairing furniture, building fishponds for his friends, and designing table games.

Adult games and entertainments were among the few hot items in the early depression years, just as they had been in previous hard times. The new, cheap cardboard jigsaw puzzles provided the craze for the winter of 1932–33; it was claimed that 100 million were sold in a six-month period.

For more complex and expensive games, the tried and true method of boosting sales was to promote them as pastimes of high society, in the hope that lower society would follow suit. Mahjong had been hyped in this way in the slump that followed World War I, and backgammon had a similar takeoff. In 1931, Parker Brothers of Salem, Massachusetts — the nation's leading games manufacturer — had invited the upper crust to well-publicized teas to promote its latest bid for stardom, Camelot, a game that combined chess and checkers with a King Arthur motif.

But Charles Darrow had a different idea. He designed a real-life game — a game that allowed the players to pretend they were tycoons; but one that was (as he explained

a few years later) typical of American business as he knew
it when he last had a job. Fortune magazine reported that
the new plaything "caters to the most grindingly acquisitive
instincts of every businessman . . . The idea is to squeeze
out all your fellow players until you own the whole board.
The more you own, the more you make."

Monopoly turned out to make plenty for Darrow, who
promptly retired to the life of a gentleman farmer, collecting the ample royalties from his invention. Parker
Brothers, who had bought the exclusive rights to Monopoly
in 1935, sold a million sets that year and has sold more
than 80 million more around the globe in the years since.
In 1974, Forbes estimated the total cumulative profit
brought in by the game at $75 million. The monopoly on
Monopoly gave Parker Brothers considerable new power
in the games market. Through the 1960s, the company required faster payments from stores, offered lower dis-
counts, and set higher prices for its games than competing
firms; if retailers didn't like the terms, they could do without
Monopoly.

By the sixties, though, business was no longer the same
as it had been when Charles Darrow last had a job. Simple
monopoly over single products was giving way to con-
glomeration. Tycoons no longer based their entire fortune
on majestic red hotels on Boardwalk and Park Place;
Sheraton Hotels was bought out by ITT. And in 1968, the
year after Charles Darrow's death, Parker Brothers became
a division of the General Mills Fun Group, Inc., a unit of
the same General Mills Corporation that offers us Betty
Crocker cake mixes and Nature Valley Granola Bars.
Whereas Parker's own foreign subsidiaries had been limited
to Canada and Western Europe, General Mills can boast of
operations in Australia, New Zealand, and Latin America as
well.

Besides Parker Brothers games and the General Mills
flours and cereals, the conglomerate makes and sells Slim
Jim beef jerky, Pennsylvania House furniture, Eddie Bauer

*sporting goods, Ship'n'Shore fashions, Gorton's seafoods,
O-Cel-O sponges, Play-Doh, Lionel model electric trains,
Star Wars toys, and more. As far as can be determined,
General Mills today owns neither St. James Place nor the
Reading Railroad. But who knows what Chance, an oppo-
nent's bankruptcy, or a few friends on Pennsylvania Avenue
might bring its way?*

Inflated Firms — and Inflated Prices

Beer is nearly as American as apple pie. As a nation, we
consume 14 million gallons of the stuff each day. In the
1930s more than 700 different companies produced a
wide variety of local brews. By 1960 two thirds of them
were gone. Today there are only forty-four different
brewers, of which the top thirteen account for 98.5 percent of the domestic output. The five largest producers —
Anheuser-Busch, Miller, Schlitz, Pabst, and Coors — control 74 percent of the market.

The beer industry is following the trend toward monopolization that has dominated the mining and manufacturing
sectors of the economy since the days of Andrew Carnegie.
It's also following the more recent trend toward conglomera-
tion. Since 1970, today's second-largest and fastest-growing
brewer, Miller, has been owned by the second-largest and
fastest-growing cigarette maker, Philip Morris.

Philip Morris brought to beer a technique, already highly
developed in the cigarette industry, known as market seg-
mentation. Once you've eliminated the authentic competition,
the way to increase your sales is to invent new needs and
products geared to specific (supposed) segments of the
population. Philip Morris has given us Virginia Slims for the
modern woman, Marlboros for the real man, Benson &
Hedges 100s for the ultrasophisticate — and Lite beer for the
less-than-serious dieter. After inundating television with commercials for Lite, Miller was making money hand over fist

selling a beer containing more water and less alcohol for a price heretofore reserved for premium brews.

Other effects of the beer industry's new look are more serious than what the nation's drinkers are imbibing this year. Purchase by conglomerates has often sounded the death knell for old, locally owned businesses, especially in the cities and towns of the Northeast. Interested in companywide goals and profit targets, the conglomerates tend to close their less profitable acquisitions, taking the loss as a tax write-off.

Pepsico, Inc., is the conglomerate built by the makers of America's second-favorite soft drink. In January 1974, Pepsico announced its intention to abandon the 119-year-old Rheingold brewery in Brooklyn, leaving 1,500 workers without jobs, health benefits, severance pay, or even accrued vacation pay. The workers charged that Pepsico had never intended to make beer, but had bought Rheingold only to get hold of its soft-drink distribution franchises.

Only a four-day sit in by 200 members of Brewery Workers locals 3 and 46 prompted Pepsico to cough up the vacation pay and look for another company willing to keep the brewery open. After intervention by New York City officials, Pepsico agreed to turn Rheingold over to the Chock Full O' Nuts company. Nonetheless, two years later the Brooklyn plant was shut down (with better severance benefits) as Chock Full O' Nuts moved all brewing to New Jersey. And in October 1977, the company was sold once again — this time to C. Schmidt and Sons of Philadelphia, which thereby became the nation's eleventh-largest brewer, producing Rheingold beer exclusively at its Philadelphia plant and preserving only the name.

What's true of beer is equally true of many basic manufacturing industries. In 1972, the year of the last major survey published by the Census Bureau, the top four companies in each industry produced 77 percent of all the auto tires, 92 percent of flat glass, 72 percent of copper, 93 percent of lead, 79 percent of aluminum, 100 percent of electric generating turbines, 75 percent of computers, 99 percent of cars, and 91 percent of locomotives. The top eight accounted for 73 percent of basic steel output, 87 percent of aircraft, and 93 percent of television production. In 1977, according to the Federal Trade Commission, the top one hundred firms owned 46 percent of the nation's total manufacturing assets.

Strictly speaking, it's true that there are few cases of actual monopoly — of a single firm controlling an entire market. Oligopoly, control by a few firms, would probably be more accurate. But the few big firms in each field long ago learned to cooperate. "GM sets the prices in the auto field, and Ford and Chrysler follow suit," points out a United Auto Workers economist. "Sure, GM could set them low enough to drive Chrysler out of business, but why bother? They make as much money selling slightly fewer cars for higher prices, and it keeps the anti-trust people off their back." The only competition that has ever come close to persuading any of the Big Three to abandon their insistence on big, expensive, rapid-obsolescence cars has come from abroad.

The dominance of the economy by a small number of large firms has a significance much larger than the stifling of competition in specific industries. Perhaps the most important economywide reflection of monopolization is the increased staying power of inflation.

There is no one simple explanation for the phenomenon of inflation. Exchanging goods and labor for money, and money for goods and labor, pervades all economic activity in this society. Therefore all the demands of every group are reflected in how much things cost. Not only wages and profits, but also pollution control, war, government services, international competition — you name it, it shows up in one way or another in prices. Much of the social conflict in society becomes a fight over what costs, and whose costs, go up.

It's a form of wishful thinking, then, to point to monopoly as the cause of inflation in the sense that without monopoly there would be no inflation. Nonetheless it has become

abundantly clear in recent years that the growth of monopolization has a lot to do with the most perplexing new
headache associated with inflation — the persistence of big
price increases well into periods of recession. The key
factor is the greater ability of monopoly corporations to follow a policy of cost-plus pricing rather than adapting their
prices to conditions in the market.

All companies try to maintain a steady quantity of profit
per item sold, aiming to set prices high enough to guarantee that, for example, 5 percent of the price of their
product goes to profits. But in an industry where many
small firms are competing for shares of the market, it's difficult to maintain such a margin in a recession period when
consumer incomes are falling. There are too many goods
for sale and not enough customers able to buy them; to
defend their shares of the market, companies will start
squeezing margins in order to offer lower prices than their
competitors. In an industry dominated by a few giant
corporations, the competition is much less intense. There
are numerous cases of conspiratorial price-fixing behind
closed doors, especially when government contracts are involved. But what's much more common is a kind of
unspoken gentlemen's agreement not to cut each others'
throats. The four or five dominant firms can limit their
output to prevent a glut, and they can keep their prices in
line.

The auto industry is a perfect example. In 1974, the auto
companies sold 29 percent fewer cars than they had the
year before. Yet prices went up as much as $1,000 a car
on some models; on the average, car prices rose 9.3 percent. As sales continued to fall, the automakers did offer
rebates in 1975. But these rebates were soon outweighed
by new price hikes. All told, car sales slumped another 6
percent in 1975, while prices rose 8.8 percent even after
the rebates were figured in. Only in 1976 did the effects of
the recession finally slow the inflation in car prices to 5.1
percent; by this time, sales were already picking up, and

the following year price increases accelerated again.

Numerous studies have demonstrated that in the industries where ownership is most concentrated in a few firms, prices have risen in each of the six recessions since World War II, whereas prices in the more competitive industries have fallen. As long as a company does not have to fear that a competitor will undercut it, what incentive does it have to lower prices?

Corporation spokespeople are usually hesitant to discuss this dynamic. A. J. Ashe, senior vice president of B. F. Goodrich — one of the big four rubber firms that produce 77 percent of the country's tires — is an exception. "It bothers me when academic economists say that price increases can't be justified because demand isn't strong enough," he told the *Wall Street Journal* in 1976. "When costs increase, prices have to go up if business is to realize the profit margins that permit new investment in facilities." The phrase "when costs increase" conjures up images of spiraling wage and raw material costs, but evidence suggests that a drop in sales is also considered a cost.

According to a study released in 1977 by the Joint Economic Committee of Congress, giant corporations increasingly try to practice what's known as mark-up pricing. In other words, first they calculate the average cost of producing one unit of their product at their current level of output and then they add whatever mark-up they need to bring their desired return on investment after all the products are sold. But when a business slump hits, the number of products sold goes down while many costs remain steady or rise; therefore, the average cost per product goes up. In order to keep total profits on target, corporations try to *increase* their mark-up. They don't always succeed, but their strategy is one that would lead to continuing high levels of inflation even in a period of recession.

Monopoly power first became important in the U.S. economy about 1900. For the previous century, when the economy was still more or less competitive, the best available evidence shows that prices went down as often as they went up. During times of scarcity, especially during wars, prices shot up, but afterward they returned to their previous level. Overall, a dollar bought as much at the end of the century as it did at the beginning.

Simultaneously with the growth of monopoly came the appearance of long-run inflation. Prices doubled during World War I; they dropped somewhat afterward, but they didn't return to their prewar level until the depths of the Great Depression. Since 1940, consumer prices have dropped in only two years: in 1949, by 1 percent; and in 1955, by less than .5 percent. The year 1980 marks the twenty-fifth year of consecutive price increases. As monopoly power increases, inflation becomes harder and harder to control.

Emperors of Energy

Of all the giant corporations, the biggest of the big are the oil companies. Year after year, five out of the top ten firms are these emperors of energy, now diversified into natural gas, coal, uranium, synthetic fuels, and even solar devices in addition to their bread-and-butter — gasoline, fuel oil, and petro-chemicals. In 1978, the number-one U.S. corporation in terms of sales was Exxon.

What's overwhelming about the oil companies is not their sheer size but their power. Energy needs and energy alternatives are at the heart of public debate and private worries to-day, and you can count on your fingers the top executives who make the crucial decisions. The energy industry illus-trates the mechanisms of monopoly corporate power as no other industry can. It brought us today's crisis and it is hard at work planning tomorrow's choices.

The Coming of the Crisis

No matter how many times you remind yourself that a bil-lion dollar-bills end to end will circle the earth four times at the equator, it's extremely difficult to reduce the ten-digit annual profit figures of Mobil or Exxon to any comprehensible human scale. But these giants do have a human face in their past — the spare, pinched face of the original John D. Rockefeller, a pioneer in the field of monopoly who put together the original Standard Oil Trust in the 1870s. By the 1880s, Rockefeller's creation refined 90 percent of the nation's oil. In the early 1900s, the family and company fortune had grown, but so had their infamy. So the family called in a young public relations man named Ivy Lee to repolish their tarnished image — Lee wrote several public service announcements explaining that the Rockefellers were really well-meaning philanthropists. (Years later, Lee went on to greater fame and fortune as the inventor of the character Betty Crocker and the slogan "Breakfast of Champions" for, yes indeed, General Mills.)

In 1911, though, federal antitrust action had broken up the Standard Oil Trust into thirty-eight separate companies. Yet the most important firms remained linked by interlocking directorates and sizable blocks of Rockefeller-owned stock, and they continued to gobble up smaller companies at will. Soon, the Rockefellers' Standard of New Jersey (now Exxon), Standard of New York (Mobil), and Standard of California (Chevron) joined with Texaco, the Mellon banking family's Gulf, and the foreign giants Royal Dutch Shell and British Petroleum (BP) to form an immensely powerful international oil cartel known in the trade as the Seven Sisters.

Beginning with a series of discussions among executives of Standard of New Jersey, Royal Dutch Shell, and British Petroleum during an ostensible grouse-shooting vacation at a Scottish castle in 1928, the major oil companies soon formalized their cartel through a pact known as the "As Is Agreement." The agreement divided up world oil markets and prevented price cutting. Each company agreed to maintain its existing share of the market and to pay a penalty to the others if it increased its share at their expense. After many years of operating under this and subsequent agreements, the major companies developed the habits of respecting each others' market shares and of expanding production in the United States or abroad only as fast as the overall growth of the market. Eventually, formal agreements may have become unnecessary, although an executive of a BP affiliate told the Senate Foreign Relations Committee that as late as 1971 he was asked to speak via international conference call to a "meeting of the chiefs," chaired by a top Exxon officer in the offices of Mobil Oil in New York.

After World War II, the Middle East and Venezuelan oil fields were intensively developed under the firm control of the Seven Sisters. In the most important country, Saudi Arabia, the oil concession was held by a joint venture known as Aramco, whose partners were Exxon, Mobil, Texaco, and Standard of California. In Iran, the U.S. companies got a share of the formerly BP-controlled wells in return for the CIA intervention that restored the Shah to power — and the oil fields to private hands — in 1953.

Even the founding of OPEC in 1960 had little effect on the Seven Sisters' control. From 1950 to 1972, the companies, reflecting the habits of the As Is Agreement days, held the growth of production in the OPEC countries to an astonishingly regular rate of 9.5 percent a year. If the companies' output in one nation rose or fell, output in other nations was adjusted to compensate.

During all these years, the companies were able to maintain the price of oil and oil products well above the actual costs of production. This was particularly true of Middle Eastern oil, because the companies had acquired long-term rights to the oil fields for relatively small royalty payments.

In the late 1960s, however, the picture began to change. The major companies experienced stagnant profits, brought about in many cases by actual declines in the returns from domestic drilling, refining, and marketing operations. One important cause was the growing share of the market supplied by independent refiners and gasoline retailers. Though these smaller firms in truth remained dependent on the major companies for much of their crude oil and even refined gasoline, they were able to compete to an extent by gaining access to some new foreign sources (especially Libyan oil) and by selling cut-rate gas at no-frills, high-volume stations in prime locations. Also, in terms of the cost of domestic production and refinery operation, the major companies were threatened by the growth of the environmental protection movement.

The companies began holding back on domestic drilling and refining as a result. "Unless and until the real nature of the crisis is understood and profit levels become such that the industry is convinced that its investments will bear fruit," Exxon treasurer Allan Hamilton declared in 1972, "the supply of energy will not be forthcoming." The small heating oil and gasoline shortages of the first half of 1973 were America's first taste of the energy crisis. The oil companies made it clear that higher prices and freedom from costly environmental restrictions were the necessary conditions for getting more oil. Yet in October of 1973 these company warnings were forgotten as the Arab members of OPEC amazed the world by ordering a temporary 25 percent cut in crude oil production and an embargo on all shipments to the United States and some European countries, as a protest against the West's support of Israel in the Middle East war. Suddenly there were long lines at gas stations in the United States. Gasoline and heating oil prices skyrocketed, and *energy crisis* became a household word. It appeared that the oil companies were no longer in the driver's seat, and that the oil shortage had not been made in New York but in Riyadh and Algiers.

Nothing could have been further from the truth. The embargo and production cut had no measurable effect on total world availability of crude oil. In 1973, production by the eleven leading members of OPEC increased at exactly its average growth rate for the preceding twenty years. Throughout 1973 and 1974, the output of the five top Middle East producers was at or above the level it would have reached by maintaining its traditional growth rate. In other words, there was no shortage of OPEC oil.

Why not? First, the production cuts were not strictly adhered to. Second, Iran (which under the Shah was a firm supporter of Israel) sharply increased production. Third, knowing that war was coming, Saudi Arabia had warned the West and allowed the production and shipment of much extra oil in the months just before the embargo. Given that there was enough crude oil, the major companies, with their undisputed control of international shipment and refining, were free to send non-Arab and even Arab oil where they wanted (through third parties). The shortages of gasoline that occurred in the United States were caused by the rate at which the companies rationed their ample stocks of oil. In March 1974, after the crisis was an established fact and the companies had won staggering price increases (and a green light for the Alaskan pipeline), they decided that cautious rationing was no longer necessary. Oil flowed freely once again.

This is not to say the relations between the oil companies and the OPEC countries were unchanged. This was a period when world oil demand was growing rapidly, the United States' ability to mount military interventions was limited by the experience of Vietnam, and some of the big domestic oil firms were trying to break the major oil companies' stranglehold on foreign sources. As a result, the bargaining power of the OPEC countries increased dramatically. All the OPEC governments (Arab and non-Arab, radical and conservative) demanded to become partners in the oil cartel, to participate in the process of controlling output and price, and to gradually take over ownership of the wells.

Willingly or not, the oil companies were quite capable of rolling with the punch. They simply passed the huge revenue increases demanded by OPEC on to consumers, and added their own mark-ups on top. During 1973, the year of the biggest OPEC increases, the companies doubled their cut on each barrel of crude imported into the United States. They also took advantage of the crisis to squeeze out independent refiners and retailers; beginning in *early* 1973 (before the embargo), they began denying crude oil and gasoline to independents on the grounds that they needed all available supplies to meet the needs of their own operations. Scot, Port, Olé, Petrol Stop, and other cut-rate independent brands vanished from the scene. Thus the companies increased their ability to profit from the "downstream" side of oil operations while sharing the "upstream" profits with OPEC.

During 1973 and 1974, the wholesale price of crude oil rose 94 percent. (This figure includes both domestic and imported oil, and reflects the mixture of price-controled domestic crude and higher-priced oil from OPEC countries that refineries were actually using.) None of the other costs of running a refinery (machinery, taxes, wages, and so on) were rising nearly as fast as the cost of crude oil. Furthermore, the major companies were refining their own oil, not buying crude on the wholesale market, so their crude oil cost probably rose less than the average wholesale price. All told, therefore, if the refiners were merely passing on the increase in crude oil costs, the prices of finished fuels would have risen significantly *less* than 94 percent.

But in fact, the wholesale prices of home heating oil and diesel fuel rose more than 140 percent during those two years, and the price of the industrial oil burned by electric utilities rose 224 percent. Only the price of gasoline — the fuel most visible to the public — rose more slowly than the price of crude and even its jump of a mere 89 percent most likely yielded substantial extra profits to the refiners.

The windfall that the oil giants reaped from their opportunity to double and even triple prices and place the whole blame on OPEC can be judged from their 1974 profit figures. From 1963 to 1972, six of the top U.S. oil companies averaged profit rates of 11 percent. In 1974, they averaged 19 percent.

These extremely high profits were only temporary, however. By 1975, it was clear that all the Western economies were either in the midst of a recession or headed in that direction. The falling incomes and cuts in industrial production that come with recession mean less consumption of oil. All of a sudden the oil shortage threatened to turn into a glut. In order to keep prices rising, the major oil companies quickly huddled with the OPEC governments to plan production cutbacks that would match the coming decline in consumption. In separate TV appearances on the CBS interview program *Face the Nation,* both Exxon chairman Clifton Garvin and Saudi Arabian oil minister Ahmed Zaki Yamani made it clear that the initiative for a 2-million-barrel-a-day cutback in Saudi production had come from the oil companies. "There hasn't been the demand," Garvin said. "As a result we've had to cut our production of oil. It's just that simple."

Meanwhile, at home, the oil shortage was rapidly replaced by a natural gas shortage. Natural gas is generally found with oil, and eighteen of the nation's top twenty producers are oil companies; the five largest natural gas producers are Exxon, Texaco, Phillips, Gulf, and Mobil. Natural gas and oil are more or less substitutable in industrial use, electrical generating, and home heating. If one fuel is significantly cheaper, buyers will tend to boycott the more expensive one. It is in the interest of the oil companies, therefore, to avoid a wide difference in prices.

In an unregulated market, the companies would have no difficulty boosting the price of natural gas up to that of oil. But since 1954, the wellhead price of natural gas piped across state lines has been regulated by the Federal Power Commission. So, sure enough, by 1975 producers were warning of an imminent shortage of natural gas, even though most estimates suggest that potentially recoverable reserves in the United States are still extensive. Production declined steadily, and much of what was produced was held off the interstate market. Warm winters staved off a crisis for two years, but when heavy snows and freezing temperatures hit the East and Midwest in January 1977, the natural gas crunch arrived. The Joint Economic Committee of Congress estimated that 2 million people suffered temporary unemployment due to the lack of gas, losing an average of $500 more in wages than they received in unemployment compensation.

Congress promptly voted to give the industry temporary relief from controls in order to get more gas into the interstate market. The companies, however, insisted that only total deregulation would provide enough incentive for them to explore for new gas. After another year and a half of congressional battles, the compromise Natural Gas Act of 1978 pledged government deregulation of most natural gas by 1985–87. In the meantime, controls were extended to cover intrastate as well as interstate gas, but the allowable price was raised by an immediate 40 percent with guaranteed additional annual increases 4 percent greater than the rate of inflation.

Finally, by the spring of 1979, we were seeing the shortage scenario repeated one more time with oil. Only the oil companies know for sure whether they conspired to create the shortage, or whether they literally held oil off the market during the crunch. But government and industry figures make it clear that, simply by following sound monopoly business practices, the companies created the situation that made the shortage possible.

In late 1977 and early 1978, the companies experienced a gasoline glut; retail prices in some cities actually dropped. Therefore, though oil remained plentiful on the world market, the companies reduced their imports, ran refineries well below capacity, and sharply reduced their stored inventories of both crude oil and gasoline. Lowering the supply in this way was good business, but in terms of insulating the United States against a possible future shortage, it was disastrous.

A minor disruption of the flow of imports caused by the revolution in Iran in January 1979 triggered the crisis, but the surprising fact is that crude oil imports during the first four months of 1979 were nearly 9 percent *higher* than they had been a year earlier. The artificial tightening of the market, not the reduction of output by striking Iranian oil workers, was the major cause of the soaring gasoline prices and reported company profits during those months.

Oil company rationing and counterproductive government

allocation programs aggravated the situation, producing a series of local and regional shortages, complete with gas lines. The shortage scare, in turn, created a climate in which oil companies' hopes for total decontrol of domestic crude oil prices blossomed. In April, President Carter began taking steps that would lead to complete decontrol by 1981. The OPEC countries, in their turn, took advantage of the tight market to declare further price hikes. But this OPEC move — singled out by the administration as the cause of shortages, inflation, and recession — merely allowed OPEC oil revenues to catch up with the rate of inflation in the United States since the big 1973–74 boost.

Bad, Worse, and Later

The above history demonstrates that the energy crisis, as we have experienced it up to now, is a creation of the oil companies. The OPEC countries have joined in as, at most, earnest imitators and junior partners. But there *is* a long-term problem of energy supply and demand.

In the United States in particular, soaring energy use is encouraged by a transportation system based on fuel-inefficient private automobiles, production processes that waste tremendous amounts of heat and are increasingly tied to oil-based synthetics and petrochemicals, a lack of recycling of energy-intensive materials such as aluminum, and antiecological building design. Sooner or later, the oil is going to run out.

Also, many oil-producing countries are trying to conserve their oil in the interest of assuring a long-term source of steady income. This is true both of OPEC leader Saudi Arabia, which is resisting the United States' pressure to hike its capacity beyond a projected plateau of 12 million barrels a day, and of non-OPEC Mexico, which wants to develop its new-found oil riches slowly.

What is the oil companies' response to this real crisis? They are happy to embrace the argument that high prices bring about conservation, but they have nothing to gain from conservation in any other form. As the price of oil rises, other forms of energy can be sold for an equivalently high price. Therefore the companies that have already monopolized oil have been turning their attention to coal, nuclear, and even solar power. Unfortunately, the alternative energy sources that they are prepared to give us — coal, nuclear power, and solar power — can best be summarized in the words bad, worse, and later.

Coal — Oil companies have been buying out coal mine operators and forming coal mining subsidiaries since they spotted the energy crisis on the horizon in the mid-1960s. Today's second-largest coal producer, Consolidation Coal, was purchased by Continental Oil in 1966. Occidental Petroleum followed suit two years later by acquiring the number-four producer, Island Creek Coal. (The largest coal company, Peabody, was recently sold by Kennecott Copper to a consortium of other leading corporations.)

Continental and Occidental, though small fry among oil companies, are nonetheless among the nation's top thirty-five industrial corporations. The large fry are not far behind. Standard of California now owns a 20-percent share of the Amax mining conglomerate, number three in coal output. Standard of Ohio is the eleventh largest coal company, and Gulf is number fifteen.

But the big story in coal is in the future, and the oil companies have devoted a large part of their effort toward snapping up as-yet-untapped reserves. A meaningful figure for the percentage of reserves held by oil companies is hard to come by. All reserve estimates are speculative, and many of the reserves lie under federal or private lands to which the mineral rights have not yet been leased. However, of the total reserves owned or leased by the 350 large and small firms listed in the *Keystone Coal Industry Manual* for 1975, fully 50 percent were in the hands of oil companies. And of the top 20 holders of coal reserves, according to the Senate Committee on Energy and Natural Resources, 11 are oil companies. The number-five coal owner in the United States is the number-one oil company, Exxon.

Though there are still big reserves of Appalachian coal, the energy companies' vision of the future is based on strip mining vast areas of the western United States. Strip mining sparsely populated regions is cheap (if the companies don't have to bear the environmental costs), and the move to the West is seen as a way to escape the power of the United Mine Workers. In 1976, strip mining produced 65 million tons of coal in the Rocky Mountain region; it was projected to yield 450 million tons by 1985. Along with the mines will come coal gasification plants and coal-fired electric plants, to produce so-called synthetic natural gas and electricity for transmission by pipeline and cable to energy-hungry cities hundreds or thousands of miles away.

These plans have met with considerable opposition from ranchers and environmentalists who fear the effect on the region's air, water, wildlife, and scenic beauty. The Four Corners coal-burning electric plant in northwestern New Mexico, for instance, in 1975 produced more daily tonnage of coal-dust particulates and sulfur dioxide than any source in any major city. (A still larger plant, called Kaiparowits, slated for southern Utah, was blocked in 1976.) The employment that comes with construction of energy plants, though touted as a big plus for local residents, brings boom-town social problems followed by an inevitable bust when construction is finished. Even the benefits for faraway cities are smaller than they look — a quarter of the electricity from Four Corners is lost in transmission before it reaches Los Angeles.

In addition, at least one third of the Western coal lies underneath the lands of peoples who, according to their treaty rights, exercise sovereignty over their resources and territory. As the energy companies have turned to Western fuel sources, they've found that a new Indian resistance is rising to meet them. Together, the twenty-two Western tribes have formed the Council of Energy-Rich Tribes (CERT), modeled on OPEC, to press for higher payments, partnerships, protection of the environment, and agreements that energy company employees will abide by Indian law.

In 1976, eighteen Navajo residents of the Four Corners area were arrested while protesting the renewal of strip mining leases with Continental. Navajo activists are now petitioning for a tribal referendum on coal mining and gasification. In the northern plains, the Northern Cheyenne have overturned leases, providing low royalties and no environmental protection, that had been granted by the federal Bureau of Indian Affairs to Continental, Chevron, and other companies. The nearby nation has forced Shell to renegotiate similar leases.

A growing sentiment is reflected by a writer from the Fort Peck (Assiniboine and Sioux) reservation in Montana, who explained, "We do not want the kind of false progress that sometimes goes under the misnomer of Economic Development . . . that strips Indian tribes of their priceless natural resources, disrupts their tradition, and leaves them only dollars which are quickly gone. We want our own kind of progress which will work for us."

Nuclear power — The oil companies have not been involved directly in the nuclear reactor business since General Atomic (a joint venture of Gulf and Royal Dutch Shell) dropped out of the reactor production field in 1976. But they are committed heavily to uranium mining and reactor fuel preparation, and they have been in the forefront of the energy industry's fruitless efforts to reprocess nuclear wastes.

Forty-eight percent of known U.S. uranium reserves are in the hands of oil companies. (These represent 72 percent of the high-quality reserves currently considered to be worth extracting.) Gulf alone controls 12 percent of known reserves, second only to Kerr-McGee, the oil-coal-nuclear firm recently found guilty of contaminating former employee Karen Silkwood with plutonium. In 1977, Gulf was exposed as a member of a secret international cartel that had brought about a sevenfold hike in uranium prices since 1972. Exxon and Continental are today leaders in uranium milling, and Exxon also operates the world's second-largest reactor fuel plant.

U.S. uranium reserves are concentrated in the states of Utah and New Mexico. Like coal, uranium is being found in increasing quantities under Indian land. In the New Mexico uranium belt, both Navajo and white miners have suffered high levels of lung cancer and other diseases as aftereffects of the first uranium boom in the 1950s. Recent studies have pinpointed dangerous levels of radiation in the waste rock piles that still dot the landscape. Despite mounting opposition, Exxon is now exploring 400,000 acres of Indian land in the Four Corners area for new deposits; Gulf is sinking the world's deepest mine shafts in search of uranium inside Mount Taylor, an area held sacred by many Navajo and Hopi people.

Eager as they have been to get the uranium out of the ground, the oil companies did not neglect the "back end" of the nuclear fuel cycle. In the late 1960s they took on the task of commercial fuel reprocessing, which was supposed to solve the nuclear industry's problems of fuel availability and waste disposal. In theory, fuel supplies could be stretched significantly by extracting (reprocessing) the unconsumed radioactive uranium from used reactor fuel rods — and the quantity of radioactive waste could be reduced in the process.

In practice, the energy companies did not demonstrate reprocessing to be feasible, and they left the taxpayers holding the bag. The first commercial facility, in West Valley, New York, was acquired by Getty Oil in 1969. Radiation leaks were common, reprocessing was not succeeding, and in 1975 Getty announced that it would close the plant rather than make investments necessary to meet new safety standards. Under the terms of an earlier agreement, New York State was responsible for storing the wastes left behind and eventually cleaning up the site.

In 1971, Gulf, Royal Dutch Shell, and Allied Chemical

formed a joint venture to build a plant of similar design, but five times larger, adjacent to an Atomic Energy Commission weapons complex in Barnwell, South Carolina. This effort was no more successful than the first and the companies offered to sell the plant to the federal government. Instead, the Carter Administration is paying them a special research subsidy to cover the costs of maintaining the unused facility, pending a future federal decision on whether to sink more funds into the search for a workable reprocessing technology.

Meanwhile, radioactive wastes continue to pile up in storage dumps — not only from reactors in this country, but from those that U.S. companies have sold abroad. None of the failures to develop effective methods of sorting or reprocessing these wastes have diminished the oil companies' enthusiasm for producing uranium and reactor fuel. Nor have they tempered the companies' public enthusiasm about nuclear power in general.

Solar power — If you've kept a close watch on energy company advertising over the past few years, you should have noticed a slow but steady increase in the attention given to solar power. We're still told that higher oil prices, less environmental regulation, and nuclear power are the energy alternatives of today, but solar energy increasingly is portrayed as an important contributor in the future.

A closer look at the industry reveals that once small companies and individual researchers have demonstrated that solar devices have potential, the big companies begin to get on the solar bandwagon. Mobil now controls the marketing arm of Tyco Labs of Waltham, Massachusetts, a pioneer in the development of photovoltaic cells, which convert sunlight directly to electricity. Exxon and Gulf also have moved into solar cell research, and Exxon and Amoco are involved in solar heating and cooling. (The aerospace companies also have shown an interest in solar technologies, particularly the most capital-intensive ones.)

In the absence of crash public programs to perfect solar electric technologies and to subsidize a changeover to solar heating, development by these major corporations is the only way that solar power is likely to get off the ground. No one else has the resources to do the job. But leaving the job in corporate hands ensures that it will be done slowly and with an eye toward the most centralized and expensive technologies.

A crucial roadblock to solar power is that on a large scale solar and nuclear methods must be viewed as mutually exclusive, economically incompatible alternatives. A nuclear electric plant and a solar electric plant both require large inputs of capital. Developing and building the plant, rather than purchasing the fuel, make up the bulk of the expense. If utilities already have nuclear plants, they're going to use less-capital-intensive coal, oil, or gas plants, not solar ones, for back-up power in times of peak demand or nuclear shutdown. And nuclear-generated electricity has a head start on solar thanks to years of federal subsidies growing out of the atomic weapons program.

All this adds up to the fact that a different mix of technologies — factory waste heat, sun, wind, and small dams, backed up by conventional fuels — will not get much of a chance until the use and development of nuclear power is stopped by a combination of political opposition and skyrocketing costs. Most likely, the giants are moving into the solar field in order to maintain their monopoly control over energy sources, but the pace of solar development will be slow as long as the nuclear option is available. According to a Senate report published in 1977, the twenty-three oil companies surveyed by investigators planned to devote just 1.1 percent of their combined research budgets to solar energy by 1980. The oil companies themselves have an interest in a continuing reliance on nuclear power long enough to reap the profits from their investment in uranium.

Futuristic solar technology is a long way from the refineries and gas stations of John D. Rockefeller, not to mention the coal-fired home heating systems that occupied the attention of young Charles Darrow. Yet the examples of price increases and policy dilemmas that result from the control of resources and production by an ever-smaller number of giant companies could go on and on. The parts of the nuclear industry that aren't tied into the oil companies, for instance, merely belong to GE and Westinghouse instead.

6.
GETTING RICH ON FOREIGN SOIL

. . . They corrupt the language and they corrupt Congress.
The bananas are left to rot on the plantations,
or rot in the freight cars by the railroad,
or are cut overripe so they are rejected
when they arrive at the dock, or are thrown into the sea;
they declare that the bunches are bruised, or too small,
or wormy, or underripe, or overripe, or rotten:
so there shall be no such thing as a cheap banana, or so
*   bananas shall be bought cheaply.*
Until there was starvation on the Atlantic coast of
*   Nicaragua.*
And the campesinos are put in jail for not selling at 30
*   centavos.*
And their bananas are bayoneted
and the Mexican Trader Steamship sinks their barges,
and the strikers are put down by shots.
(And the Nicaraguan deputies are invited to a garden
*   party.)*
But the Negro has seven kids to look after.
And you have to do something. You have to eat.
And you have to take what they pay you. 24 centavos a
*   bunch.*
Meanwhile the subsidiary company Tropical Radio sends a
*   cablegram to Boston:*
"We hope that the distribution we have made
among the deputies of the majority party in Nicaragua
will have the approval of Boston

because of the incalculable benefits it represents for the
   Company."
And from Boston to Galveston by telegram
and from Galveston by cable and telegram to Mexico
and from Mexico by cable to San Juan del Sur
and from San Juan del Sur by telegram to Puerto Limón
and from Puerto Limón by canoe to the jungle
the order of the United Fruit Company arrives:
"The United is not buying any more bananas."
And they fire the workmen in Puerto Limón.
The small factories close down.
No one can pay their debts.
And the bananas are rotting in the freight cars by the
   railroad.
   So there shall be no such thing as a cheap banana
   and so bananas shall be bought cheaply. — 19 centavos
   a bunch.
The workers get scrip instead of a day's wages.
Instead of a salary, debts.
And the plantations are abandoned as they are now no use
   for anything
and given over to colonies of the unemployed.
                . . .

"He is a bandido," Somoza said, "a bandolero."
And Sandino never sold anyone's property.
Which, being translated, means
that Somoza called Sandino a gangster.
And Sandino never stole anyone's property.
And Moncada called Sandino a bandit at public banquets
and in the mountains Sandino didn't have any salt,
and his men were shivering with cold in the mountains,
and he had mortgaged his father-in-law's house
to set Nicaragua free while in the Presidential palace
Moncada had mortgaged the whole of Nicaragua.
"It's obvious that he isn't" — the American minister said
laughing

— *"but it's in the technical sense that we call him a*
bandolero."
What is that light in the distance? Is it a star?
It's Sandino's light as he moves through the dark of the
forest.
That's where he is with his men around their red bonfire
wrapped in their blankets with rifles on their shoulders
smoking or singing sad songs from the north,
none of them stirring, only their shadows stirring.

>   —From "La hora cero" ("Zero Hour"), by the
>   Nicaraguan poet Ernesto Cardenal

We are taught in school that the Age of Empires has come
and gone, replaced by a new era of more equal interdepen-
dence among nations. But last year, when Nicaraguan
dictator Anastasio Somoza finally faced up to the fact that his
family's forty-three-year reign was over, the person to whom
he conveyed his decision to resign was none other than the
U.S. ambassador. ("He may be a son of a bitch," good
neighbor Franklin Roosevelt once remarked about this
Somoza's father, "but he's our son of a bitch.")

Outright colonies, it's true, have largely disappeared,
though such notable exceptions as Northern Ireland and
Puerto Rico have yet to gain their independence. But the system of political and economic domination of the former colonies by the industrial powers of Europe, the United States,
and Japan is still very much in evidence, whether you look at
the catalogues of foreign operations contained in corporate
reports or at the products of our consumer society. Try imagining the banana split without United Fruit Company's
Central American plantations or auto trim without Union Car-
bide's Rhodesian chrome mines.

In Asia, Africa, and Latin America, even the middle-of-the-
road politicians refer to this system by the name of *imperialism*. Its many economic facets include the extraction of raw
materials, the scramble for low-cost manufacturing sites, and

the reaping of ever-growing quantities of interest from foreign loans. But the heart of most Third World economies is agriculture; the most pressing problem for their people is finding enough food. Therefore, this chapter will examine the effect of economic imperialism on the world's food and agriculture.

Why World Hunger?

The United Nations has estimated that 450 million people, worldwide, were seriously malnourished in 1976. The World Bank put the figure closer to 1 billion. Whatever the correct figure, millions of people live so close to the edge of starvation that droughts, wars, and floods produce immediate famines.

Usually, the problem of hunger is explained by saying that the world's population is outstripping its ability to produce food. That's a tidy, but false explanation. On a world scale, food production has been growing a little *faster* than population. Between 1967 and 1976, food production per person rose an average of 0.5 percent a year.

Grain crops — the world's basic source of food — have done better. Between 1969 and 1976, the average increase in grain harvested per person was 1.7 percent a year, despite the bad harvests of 1972 and 1974.

In simplest terms, the problem is that the productive grain fields of the world are not distributed the same way as the people. Most countries have to import grain, and *only* the United States, Canada, Australia, sometimes Argentina and New Zealand export it. What makes the United States, Canada, and Australia special is their history. A crucial part of that history is the settlement of all three countries by Europeans who killed or drove off the indigenous peoples. The Europeans then found themselves in possession of vast amounts of land and of the resources to develop it through increasingly mechanized agriculture.

Today, the United States is grain dealer to the world. As

former U.S. ambassador to the U.N. John Scali put it a few years ago, "The U.S. is to food what Iran, the Arab states, and Venezuela are to oil." We are the only country to export all the basic food grains and soybeans; we sell 70 percent of the world market's corn, 40 percent of the wheat, 20 percent of the rice, and 80 percent of the soybeans.

Of course, to say that "we" do the exporting is something of a euphemism. Four giant grain companies actually dominate the grain trade. Cargill, Continental, Bunge, and Dreyfus are not household names. But even before the grain is harvested, they've arranged to buy it from farmers; store it in their grain elevators; transport it in their barges, freight cars, and trans-oceanic ships; and market it through their export firms. They have expanded into the food manufacturing business as well; their holdings include bakeries, livestock feed processors, chicken and hog farms, and even fast-food outlets.

Held by single super-rich families, these grain giants are not required to make their profit or sales figures public. Still, Department of Agriculture figures on export values give a sense of the companies' enormous wealth and power. In 1977, export companies' grain and soybean sales totaled $13.5 billion. Cargill alone, according to *Business Week*, accounts for more overseas sales than any other U.S. company.

But what about the vast nonindustrial regions of the "Free World"? Why don't they produce enough to feed themselves? The secret of their failure, like the secret of U.S. success, lies in their colonial history. In Asia and many parts of Africa, Europeans didn't take the land from the native peoples. In some cases, instead, they took the people themselves. The U.S. economy, particularly, was built on cotton farming in the South and cotton mills in the North — all made possible by the labor of slaves stolen from Africa. In other cases, they took the fruits of the native people's labor. The wealth produced in the mines and farms of the colonies, as well as in the slave trade, made possible the rapid industrialization of the home countries and the settler states. But the process by which the wealth was extracted left the colonies stranded on a road to nowhere.

In agriculture, the imperial powers insisted that the colonies produce nonessential crops for the world market, rather than food for local consumption. The proceeds from all crops went to Europe and North America. Today, the Third World countries produce surpluses only of nonstaple crops — coffee, tea, cocoa, tobacco, rubber, jute, cotton. If people could live on cocoa, Ghana would be doling out food aid to the United States.

The destruction of the colonies' self-sufficiency was pioneered by the British in India. Before its conquest for the good of the British East India Company in the eighteenth century, India was a rich country, an exporter of both grain and finished textiles. Two centuries of British rule turned it into an impoverished importer of grain and manufactured goods. A lesser-known example, which we'll examine in detail, is the history of the West African lands bordering the Sahara Desert that are called, in Arabic, the *Sahel* ("fringe"). The mass media discovered the people of the Sahel countries as tragic victims when 100,000 of them starved to death in the drought and famine of the early 1970s. But they did not reveal the roots of this tragedy in French colonialism, nor its perpetuation today by U.S. and French agribusiness.

The Making of a Famine

In the mid-nineteenth century, the people of the Sahel region (see map) farmed according to methods well adapted to the climate. In the driest lands, nomads drove herds of livestock over vast areas, taking advantage of seasonal variations in rainfall and vegetation. The herds included a careful balance of different types of animals (camels and goats as well as cattle) suited to different sources of food. Farmers left some desert land fallow for up to twenty years between plantings. Everywhere, they used a variety of crops to maintain soil quality. Food crops included rice, corn, and millet. In what is now Mali, villages maintained granaries to store surplus grain from good harvests in preparation for years of drought.

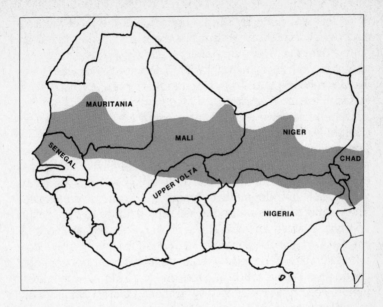

The shaded area indicates that part of Africa known as the Sahel,
or fringe of the desert.

Then came the French, advancing eastward from their ini-
tial colony in Senegal under a policy of "peace or gun-
powder." The last two decades of the nineteenth century
were marked by continuous warfare in the Sahel. By 1900,
France had an African empire. Immediately, the French promoted specialization in a few crops: cotton (for use by French
manufacturers trying to compete with British textiles), peanuts (to be processed into oil), and beef (which Europeans
preferred to camel meat). These goods were intended for
export to France, not for use in the colonies. Any revenue
that stayed in the colonies was used to build railroads to get
the goods out, not irrigation systems or other improvements
in agriculture.

The cheapest way to acquire these export goods, the
French found, was to force the peasants to grow them. Some-

times this was done by simple decree, but the most favored method was taxation. Peasants were made to pay taxes on land, buildings, and even family members. These taxes had to be paid in francs; the only way to acquire francs was to sell the desired crops to French trading companies. The system was simple, and it worked.

The effects were all the more severe because the trading companies, as the sole buyers in their areas, could severely depress prices. The lower the prices and the higher the taxes imposed by colonial authorities to finance their own operations, the more the peasants had to grow. This pressure forced the abandonment of traditional farming techniques. The people of the area began selling the future to pay for the present. Pasture and forest lands were plowed and water-saving methods of cultivation were abandoned. Intensive cotton cultivation depleted the soil, leaving it too poor for food production when cotton moved on. Nomads (whose movements were now restricted by artificial colonial boundaries) raised only cattle and resorted to overgrazing in order to pay their taxes.

The much-publicized advance of the desert followed — not a natural calamity, but one created by colonialism. By the time the Sahel countries gained independence in the 1960s, many lands were depleted, the peanut oil market had plummeted, and the peasants were deeply in debt. Former U.S. ambassador to Upper Volta Elliot Skinner has concluded that "the plight of the nations in the Sudan-Sahel zone is a direct result of a colonial policy that treated these areas as a plantation for export crops and as a reservoir for manpower to feed France's colonial armies."

The arrival of political independence might have led to a new type of development, but in fact it did not. Colonialism created a class structure intricately linked to its ways, and this class structure has not been overturned. Local elites of land-owners, tax collectors, government functionaries, and food traders now live off the export-oriented agriculture and continue to encourage it. The taxes also continue; in 1970, Mali's tax forced each small farmer to deliver 106 pounds of cotton. In the years of the drought, as peasants borrowed and then sold their harvests cheaply, traders and moneylenders prospered. Sahelian towns now feature *chateaux de la sécheresse*, "mansions of the drought," homes of the local elite that for the first time rival in splendor the homes of the wealthy Europeans there.

The amazing fact is that the famine of the early 1970s could have been avoided, if the export business could have been interrupted. In researching their book *Food First*, Frances Moore Lappé and Joseph Collins found that every Sahel country except mineral-rich Mauritania actually was producing enough food to carry its population through the drought. The Sahel is a net exporter not only of peanuts but of barley, beans, fresh vegetables, beef, and fish, despite protein malnutrition among its children that, even in normal years, is about the worst in the world. During the drought, as relief foods came in, local produce went out — sometimes on the same ships and planes. In Mali, peanut and rice exports actually reached new highs. Sahelian cattle exports rose 41 percent between 1968 and 1971.

Credit for this absurd situation should go not only to the French colonizers and the local elite, but to U.S. and European agribusinesses, which not only carry on the export operations but increasingly are establishing their own plantations. These agribusinesses have brought some new developments in farming, but no food to feed the hungry. An example is Bud Antle, Inc., a California-based vegetable grower and marketer. In 1972, about the time United Farm Workers leader Cesar Chávez was jailed in California for defying a no-strike court injunction secured by Bud Antle, the corporation was forming a joint enterprise with the Senegalese government known as Bud Senegal.

Bud Senegal grows vegetables on its own plantation, using a drip-irrigation system whose plastic tubes individually water each plant continuously. The idea is to eliminate the peasant producers entirely, replacing them with a type of plantation

agriculture that requires very few hired laborers. Few peasants got jobs on Bud's operation and many were hurt when
Bud, in laying out its plantation, uprooted the baobab trees
that villages had been treating as common property. The
trees had provided rope, building materials, fuel, and wind
erosion protection.

Bud's irrigation system was financed by the Senegalese
government. The World Bank also provided a loan to the new
venture, one of only three loans the bank made to private
businesses in 1974. Bud Senegal is supposed to be a show-
case development project. Yet all production is for Europe,
where it is flown by jet. The Senegalese themselves can't afford Bud products. In 1974, as Senegalese starved,
European governments were reacting to a vegetable glut at
home by buying up and destroying $53 million worth of
produce to stabilize prices. Bud Senegal has even destroyed
green beans on its plantations when European prices are too
low to justify the expense of shipment. The defense offered by
a Bud representative is that "Senegalese are not familiar with
green beans and don't eat them."

In July 1977, the Senegalese government took over Bud
Senegal. But beyond providing new high-level jobs for the
country's elite, the company's policies have not changed. Bud
Antle still controls the export end of the business. And domestically, Bud Senegal is taking over the sale of small farmers'
crops; half of all produce sold in the capital city is sold at Bud
stands.

At the same time, Bud Antle has been moving into Gambia,
Nigeria, the Ivory Coast, and Mali and intends to expand into
the rest of West Africa as well. In February 1978, Bud Antle
merged into the giant agribusiness firm of Castle and Cooke,
creating a truly worldwide empire. Castle and Cooke, parent
company of Dole Pineapple, is based in Hawaii and owns
operations from Thailand to Puerto Rico. Its products include
mushrooms, tuna fish, sugar, beer, bananas, and canned
fruits as well as fertilizer, swimming pool equipment, and steel
pipe.

Thanks to the wonders of agribusiness, the most advanced agricultural techniques now coexist with the most miserable poverty. There is no going back to the precolonial days. The countries of the Third World now need to develop their agriculture so they can feed their people. In *Food First,* Lappé and Collins estimate that it would be physically possible for the Sahel region to increase its production sixfold to become the "breadbasket of Africa," thanks to extensive underground lakes and an excellent sunny growing season.

The question is, what type of development is going to be pursued? Can a modern agriculture make use of the human and physical resources that exist? Can it deliver jobs, income, and food to the peasants, landless laborers, and the growing number of people pushed off the land into urban slums? And what role can the public in the developed countries play in encouraging humane, balanced development in the Third World?

With Friends Like These . . .

The U.S. government agency charged with answering these questions is the Agency for International Development, aptly initialed AID. The key foreign aid unit in Washington, AID is devoted — according to the fiscal 1979 federal budget — to "helping developing nations meet the basic human needs of their poor through programs designed to produce growth and equity." It is specifically directed to make low-interest loans to programs that "directly address world problems of hunger and malnutrition."

Sounds good, doesn't it? But the sad reality is that the only needs AID succeeds in addressing are those of the agribusiness companies and the local elites.

Take as an example an outfit known as the Latin American Agribusiness Development Corporation (LAAD). By 1976, LAAD had pulled in $17 million of those low-interest loans, at rates of 3 to 4 percent. LAAD is a private, profitmaking company founded in 1970 by the Bank of America to develop and finance Central and South American agribusinesses. The fifteen partner firms include, besides the big bank, Ralston Purina, the grain giant Cargill, the John Deere super-tractor firm, and Bud Antle's parent firm, Castle and Cooke.

In 1975 alone, LAAD's net profit was $500,000, on a total capital investment by the corporate partners of only $2 million. This lucrative return comes largely from luxury export operations such as beef, frozen vegetables, and even flowers. According to a consulting firm hired by AID to evaluate LAAD in 1974, "The bulk of the product lines handled are either destined for upper middle, upper class consumption, or for export."

Nonetheless, AID has continued to fund the agribusiness consortium. One of LAAD's favorite locales is Nicaragua, where it has interests in cattle ranches and supermarkets. It has also loaned more than $300,000 to a Nicaraguan company called Industrias Amolonca, owned by relatives of the Somozas, which ties up prime agricultural land to produce black-eyed peas and freezing vegetables for Safeway and Seven-Eleven stores.

Officially, AID identifies small farmers rather than agribusiness as the target group for many of its projects. The goal in such projects is to encourage these farmers to produce more food for the market, increasing their efficiency through use of machinery, "miracle" seeds, and scientific techniques. These small farmers are not targeted because they are the hungriest; they are targeted because there is a possibility that some of them could become members of a stable, conservative, landholding class.

Such farmers are not the really poor in most underdeveloped countries. The really poor are those who own little or no land and cannot afford to buy food even when it is available. For them, increased mechanization means only that they'll have less chance to eke out a living as seasonal farmworkers and less chance to work as tenant farmers on land that the owners were formerly unable to till themselves. AID spokesperson Robert Nooter admitted as much to the Congress in

1977, when he said, "We recognize that increased productivity by small farmers will not by itself assure an adequate diet for the poor majority."

Moreover, much of the aid for small farmers finds its way into the hands of the larger farmers — the rural rich. This happens in part because of the political power of the larger farmers, but also because of the type of projects that AID finances. Road building and rural electrification, for instance, loom large in AID's "food" aid. But an electrical outlet is useful only to the farmer who is rich enough to buy something to plug into it. A $125 million electrification project being carried out by AID in Indonesia, according to the agency's administrator there, will result in the better-off farmers becoming able to mill their own rice with electric milling machines. Poor farmers won't be able to afford the machines; and, the AID man admitted to questioners, the landless laborers who used to do the milling will face higher unemployment.

Likewise, roads are of little use to the really small farmers, who don't have much extra food to send to market. But they are quite handy for larger farmers and foreign plantation owners. According to two University of Washington researchers who studied AID's plan for a $55 million interregional highway in Liberia, "It may well make it easier for Firestone vehicles to traverse the country, but its relationship to the small farmer's economic and social benefits, the avowed goals, is non-existent." Firestone Corporation operates large rubber plantations in Liberia.

In practice, then, U.S. aid reinforces not only the dominance of foreign interests but the gaps between rich and poor in the underdeveloped countries as well. AID can offer to the poor only nutritional education and occasional U.S. surplus commodities. As anger over the unequal distribution of food has mounted in the Third World, development experts in the capitalist countries have increasingly turned their attention to population control.

"The Self-Interest Thing"

Many supporters of population control as a solution to the problems of hunger may be quite sincere about their efforts, but the essence of this prescription is to give the appearance of addressing social problems while leaving the class structures and corporate domination of the underdeveloped countries entirely unchallenged. It is a method of solving problems at the expense of the people who have them.

This logic is not lost on the U.S. government, which since the mid-1960s has been an avid promoter of birth control in poor countries. Dr. R. T. Ravenholt, director of AID's Office of Population, told the *St. Louis Post-Dispatch* quite frankly in 1977 that an important function of population control is to maintain "the normal operation of U.S. commercial interests around the world. . . . Without our trying to help these countries with their economic and social development," he went on, "the world would rebel against the strong U.S. commercial presence. The self-interest thing is a compelling element."

Between 1969 and 1972 AID's spending for population programs abroad soared from $34 million to $123 million, while its health expenditures dropped from $164 million to $60 million. In recent years, AID has spent more on population control programs than on agriculture and rural development combined. Increasingly, the population establishment is turning to sterilization as its favorite method of reducing births. "Of the four billion people in the world," Dr. Ravenholt told Congress in 1976, "half live in the developing countries, not counting the People's Republic of China. Approximately one-fifth of these, 400 million, are women of reproductive age. It is likely that more than 100 million additional couples in the developing countries will accept sterilization during the next decade if the services are made fully available."

Arranging for the sterilization of one quarter of the fertile women in the Third World sounds like quite a feat, but the U.S. government has had considerable practice. In Puerto Rico — a U.S. colony, under various guises, since its capture

from Spain in 1898 — sterilization programs have been
under way since the 1930s. According to the island's Department of Health, approximately 35 percent of Puerto Rican
women of child-bearing age had been sterilized as early as
1965; two-thirds were still in their twenties. The Committee
for Action on Latin America reports that, by now, 44 percent
of the women with family incomes under $5,000 have been
sterilized. Needless to say, poverty has not been eliminated
by this practice.

The real hope for feeding the people of the Third World is a
path of development based on economic independence,
transformation of internal class structures, and redistribution
of income. But radical change in Africa, Asia, and Latin
America is what the U.S.–based multinational corporations
want the least. It should come as no surprise that AID funds
are also used as a weapon against radical insurgency. Despite
the "human rights" rhetoric of the Carter Administration, AID
money flows most copiously to the right-wing dictatorships
that outlaw opposition in order to preserve the power of privileged elites.

In sub-Saharan Africa, for instance, General Mobuto Sese
Seko's corrupt military regime in Zaire has been one of the
top two recipients of U.S. economic aid since 1976. In Latin
America, Chile led the list in 1975 and 1976; when international outcries against the Pinochet dictatorship's routine use
of torture forced a cut in U.S. aid to Chile, the nearby military
regime of General Hugo Banzer in Bolivia took its place. In
Asia, Indonesia has been the leading aid recipient, and funds
for the martial-law government of Philippine President
Ferdinand Marcos have grown steadily.

The story of Chile has been told often enough: U.S. economic aid was almost entirely cut off from 1970 to 1973 while
the popularly elected socialist government of Salvador
Allende was instituting a program of full employment, nationalization of foreign-owned industry, land reform, and increased services and political power for the poor. Aid was

restored only after the military seized power, murdered Allende and thousands of his supporters, reopened the door to U.S. corporations and imposed a drastic austerity program on the Chilean people.

The example of Thailand is not so well known. In 1973, the ruling military dictatorship was overthrown in the wake of a student uprising. A civilian government promised political and economic reforms; the United States responded by reducing economic aid to $7 million in fiscal 1975, while continuing to hand over $40 million to the military. The armed forces regained power in a bloody coup the following year, and economic assistance was doubled.

Elsewhere in Asia — in the Philippines — AID funding has risen more than fivefold since 1972 despite dramatic increases in political imprisonment and torture. Strikes have also been outlawed since 1972, gladdening the hearts of U.S. firms, including Castle and Cooke, which moved much of the Dole Pineapple growing and canning operation from Hawaii to the Philippines in the 1960s to escape unions.

Modernization in Sunny São Paulo

Anyone who follows the increasing numbers of industrial plant closings in the United States can see that the interests of multinational corporations in the Third World go far beyond what can be taken out of the soil. In recent decades, containerized shipping, computerized recordkeeping, and more and more routinized production processes have given the multinationals a lot of freedom to spread their factories around the world. At the same time, hunger and unemployment in the Third World countryside have driven many people to city slums, creating a pool of workers who must accept factory jobs at wages only a fraction of what corporations would have to pay their employees in the United States, Germany, or Japan.

So General Electric closes its appliance-timer plants in Massachusetts and sets up shop in Singapore instead; Motorola pulls up stakes in Arizona and relocates just south of the border in Mexico. The runaway shop phenomenon, long familiar within the United States, has been internationalized. At home, that means large layoffs of workers in a number of older manufacturing industries; the threat of moving also gives corporations another valuable bargaining chip in labor negotiations. But bad as this is for workers here, has the extension of industry brought about a better life in the Third World?

The answer is no. Take Brazil, often touted as an economic miracle — a Third World country that, with the help of foreign corporate investment, was rapidly becoming an industrial power. In the late sixties and early seventies, exports boomed and the economic growth rate stood at an impressive 10 percent a year. The boom was cut short by the sudden quadrupling of world oil prices in 1973, but for the majority of Brazilians it had been a fraud all along. The limits were made clear even to outsiders by the publication of Brazil's 1970 census data a few years ago.

What the growth of industry brought to Brazil was an extremely privileged, wealthy minority with the living standards of a developed country, coexisting with an impoverished majority in the countryside and in the slums and shantytowns of the cities. Between 1960 and 1970, the top 5 percent of the population *increased* their share of the national income from 27 percent to 37 percent; the bottom 80 percent of the people saw a decline of their share of the income from 45 percent to 37 percent.

The high growth rates of the miracle years meant little to the industries making goods for the majority of people. Production of clothing and shoes, for instance, increased only 1 percent from 1969 to 1972 — and a rising share of that production was destined for overseas markets. Rather, the boom was based on production of luxury goods for the Brazilian elite and for export. Chief among these were private cars, built at the local plants of Ford, Volkswagen, General Motors, Chrysler, Mercedes, and other multinationals.

What about the workers in these factories? Number one, they represent only a drop in the bucket compared to the masses of the poorest Brazilians. Number two, they did not benefit from the profits of the boom. Real wages for industrial workers (both the minimum wage and the average wage) were lower in 1970 than in 1960. These statistics reflect the economic strategy of the military dictatorship that has ruled Brazil since seizing power with U.S. support in 1964. One of the new regime's first acts, aimed at improving the climate for foreign investment, was to bring labor unions under strict government control.

In 1978, however, a slight loosening in that control unleashed a wave of illegal auto strikes which in turn spread to other workers including teachers, bus drivers, and bank employees. In May 1979, workers battled police for possession of union headquarters in the industrial suburbs surrounding the major manufacturing center of São Paulo. Despite the government's dispatch of tanks and troops to occupy factories and public gathering places, strikers remained off the job until significant concessions were granted. This changed climate may be giving the multinationals some new thoughts. Volkswagen do Brasil (VW's second largest foreign subsidiary) has announced plans for new production facilities in Egypt and South Africa.

7.
TRADE WARS, OR WHY TOYOTA MEANS MORE THAN TRANSPORTATION

At the close of World War II, British troops occupied a half-built city in central Germany which the Nazis had called die Stadt des Kraft-durch-Freude Wagen, *"the city of the Strength-through-Joy car." The centerpiece of the town was a factory that had been built to apply American assembly-line methods to the production of millions of small, cheap, efficient cars that were supposed to be the Führer's offering to German workers.*

Strength-through-Joy was the name of the Nazi-controlled workers' organization that had replaced the outlawed labor unions. In 1938, Hitler had announced a special lay-away plan under which workers could volunteer for a weekly payroll deduction that, after four years, would in theory entitle them to one of the new cars. Workers who couldn't keep up the payments, though, would lose their money.

The car itself had been designed in the early 1930s by the noted Austrian auto engineer Ferdinand Porsche, but European automakers had rejected the idea of a cheap mass-market car. Porsche's "volkswagen" had found no serious takers until the Nazis — eager to make Germany a motorized nation like the United States — had seized on it. Porsche had been appointed Reich Auto Designer and been sent to the United States to recruit German-born technicians away from Ford and other U.S. firms. But plans for the rechristened Strength-through-Joy car were interrupted by the war, and the new plant was put to work

making jeeps, mines, V-1 flying bombs, and other war
material.

When the British arrived in 1945, the building had been
partially destroyed by bombing raids, but the machinery
was largely intact. Allied military personnel had learned
during the war to admire the German jeeps, powered by
air-cooled engines mounted in the rear. They were, in fact,
modified Volkswagens. The British put the plant back into
operation in order to provide work for the local populace
(swelled by growing numbers of refugees from the nearby
Russian zone) and to produce cars for the occupation
forces. Meanwhile, they tried to find an Allied manufacturer who wanted to take it over. A commission of
British experts led by Rolls-Royce executives was simply
not interested. GM and Ford already had their own
German subsidiaries (Opel and Ford Werke), which they
had been operating since the prewar years; a top executive told Henry Ford that the Nazi plant was "not worth a
damn." Finally, in 1949 it was turned over to the new West
German government, which organized the Volkswagen
business as a privately operated corporation supervised by
the state.

By 1956, the new company had turned out its millionth
Volkswagen and was producing and selling four times as
many cars annually as Ford Werke. Given the low level of
German industrial wages at the time, only 5 percent of
VW's workers owned any kind of car, but export markets
were booming. The company was claiming to be the
world's single largest exporter and had set up assembly
plants in Mexico, Brazil, South Africa, Ireland, and Belgium
as well. In the United States, the small car with the twenty-
year-old design was outselling all other foreign models
combined; while Detroit's sales were dropping, VW was
making steady gains.

The Wall Street Journal wrote wonderingly about the
"utilitarian miniature cars" and wondered "how long VW
can get away with its refusal to restyle." "But so far," the

business paper noted, "the public has not complained." In 1960, Detroit introduced the first compact cars in an attempt to regain lost ground, but VW's sales continued to rise. By 1968, the basic beetle was the eighth most popular car model in the United States and Americans made up a third of the company's customers. With VW's sales as big as Chrysler's, there was now a Big Four, rather than a Big Three, in the world auto market.

With big-time status, however, came big-time problems. Despite its importation of production workers from lower-wage Italy (housed in a special Italian "village" near the major plant) VW no longer enjoyed the low labor costs of the past. The rising value of the German mark relative to the dollar also boosted costs while cutting income. And in 1971 — the year that total cumulative production of the VW beetle surpassed that of the Model-T Ford — the company was shocked to find that U.S. customers were buying nearly as many Japanese cars as VWs.

Undaunted, the German firm followed a path well known in American board rooms: when in doubt, run. In 1974, it announced that all further expansion of production would take place outside Europe. Much of the expansion was slated for the Third World, particularly Brazil, but the United States was hardly forgotten. VW began selling Rabbit engines to Chrysler for use in American cars in 1976; in 1978 it opened its own Rabbit assembly plant in Pennsylvania. (The labor climate here was not so mild as VW had hoped, however. Six months after its opening, the plant was shut down by an unexpected strike. Workers chanted "No Money, No Bunny," insisting on a contract that put their wages closer to those paid by the Big Three in Detroit.)

VW's recently announced plans include an engine factory and another assembly plant somewhere in North America, as well as other expansions in South America, Africa, and Asia. At home, it plans to sink $4 billion into automating existing plants. In June 1979, the U.S. business community was even abuzz with rumors that the German firm was about to buy out

*Chrysler. Rejected out of hand by the U.S. and British auto
industries thirty years ago, VW today is a major multinational
corporation. It is a symbol of the ever-shifting pattern of
competition and cooperation among the capitalist industrial
powers — a pattern that more and more dominates today's
economic news.*

In the late 1940s, the United States was sitting on top of the
world. It was the undisputed leading military power, the only
nation to build and use an atomic bomb. Equally important
was U.S. economic superiority. American business had
emerged from the war with its industrial capacity, transportation and communications systems, financial reserves, and
labor force intact. The war-torn economies of enemies and
allies alike, on the other hand, were hungry for U.S. investment funds and goods.

The only problem with being on the top is that there's
nowhere to go but down. The decades of relative prosperity
that followed the war were based on an international position
that was by its very nature temporary. The international business boom created by rebuilding from the war could not go
on forever; eventually the world economy would stop
growing so fast. And the reconstruction of the Japanese and
European economies had to bring increased competition for
U.S. corporations. The problems faced by the United States
today, though rooted in the dynamics of the domestic economy, have been intensified by the darkening international
situation.

This underlying reality is easy to describe and to grasp. Yet
the technical details of trade relations and international currency exchange are light-years removed from everyday
economic experience. This area of economics remains the
most mysterious to nonexperts. This chapter will try to shed
some light by discussing: first, the growth of foreign competition; second, the emergence and the meaning of balance-of-
trade and balance-of-payments deficits; and, finally, the
impact of international events on the domestic economy.

The Rise of Competition

In the late 1940s, it was in the interest of U.S. business to re-build the economies of Europe and Japan in order to create markets for domestically produced goods and opportunities for profitable foreign operations. Politically, it was also important to create strong anti-communist allies. Government and private funds poured into reconstruction.

At first, the danger of competition from these recovering in-dustrial economies was small. Remember the 1950s jokes about cheap Japanese imports — crummy little toys, shoddy fabrics, trinkets with fake "made in USA" labels? Yet some-how, by 1978, Japan had built the world's most modern, automated steel factories and the most functional cars; in early 1978, Japan was selling $1 billion more goods a *month* to the United States than the United States was selling to Japan.

In explaining Europe's and Japan's rise to competitiveness, much has been made of the opportunity for modernization provided by the destruction of their old industrial facilities by war. Yet recent studies estimate that German industrial capa-city right after the war was greater than it had been in 1936, when Germany was the world's second-largest industrial power. German industry expanded very rapidly during the war, just as U.S. industry did, and only about 25 percent of its capacity was destroyed by war damage and immediate post-war dismantling.

As least as important in explaining the "economic miracles" performed in both Germany and Japan during the 1950s and 1960s is the area of internal class relations. In Germany, though much of the physical plant and equipment survived, the social and economic organization had been shattered. Transportation, communication, and currency circulation had collapsed. The population was temporarily reduced to near-starvation levels. German workers remained highly trained and skilled, but their trade union militance had been conveniently destroyed by twelve years of fascism. Their bargaining position was further reduced by the influx into the labor force of many of the 12 million refugees from East Germany.

So the German miracle consisted of putting experienced workers to work in existing plants at an extremely high rate of exploitation. In 1955, the average male German worker worked eight hours more per week than his counterpart in the United States. In 1956, West German real wages were no higher than they had been back in 1938. By the time German wages caught up even with those in neighboring countries, in about 1960, a decade of immensely profitable expansion had prepared German companies to move on to a new stage, based on more mechanization on one hand, and the employment of cheap immigrant labor from southern Europe and northern Africa on the other.

In Japan, because of peculiarities of history and class structure, the working class had never won many of the elementary victories achieved in other countries. Despite occasional strike waves and riots, workers were largely unrepresented by unions, and there was little social legislation to protect them. Immediately after the war, there was a rapid rise in union membership and activity and in the strength of left-wing political parties. But this movement ran into the combined opposition of Japanese business and the temporary military government imposed by the U.S. armed forces that occupied Japan after Hirohito's surrender.

Led by General Douglas MacArthur, the U.S. authorities maneuvered against the unions and left-wing parties, banned two general strikes, and played an active part in the destruction of the larger, more militant, of the two union federations. With the end of the military occupation in 1952, Japanese unions gained strength; but the share of the Gross National Product going to wages has remained smaller than in the United States or Europe. Social security and pension programs even today are meager by U.S. and European standards; as a result, Japanese workers must save a larger share of their incomes (25 percent after taxes between 1973 and 1977, compared to 7 percent in the United States and 15 percent in West Germany), providing banks with a larger pool of money to lend to businesses for new investments. Also, until recently, there were almost no laws requiring business to invest in pollution-control devices.

For business, though, the Japanese government carries out a wide range of services. Detailed planning for the growth of the larger firms and most profitable industries, protection from foreign competition, loans, tax exemptions, research subsidies, and more are provided. The level of government and business cooperation in Japan is analagous to what exists in the United States between the government and the aerospace industry. In Japan, as in Germany, the later years of the postwar boom brought rising wages and a need for a new strategy. The government has encouraged Japanese companies to move their labor-intensive industries, such as textiles, to South Korea, Taiwan, and Southeast Asia, and to concentrate on more technological products at home.

Fiddling All the Way to the Bank

What were U.S. companies doing while Japanese and German businesses were regaining their strength? First, they were *becoming* foreign competitors themselves. Second, they were concentrating on making the most money they could in the short run, in ways that actually undercut their ability to compete later on.

U.S. expansion abroad since World War II has been based far more on investment than on trade. U.S. firms had only $12 billion worth of foreign investments in 1950. By 1960, that number had climbed to $32 billion; by 1970, $75 billion; and by 1977, $149 billion. In 1976–77 about a quarter of all U.S. corporate profits, after taxes, came from abroad. The bulk of that income came from foreign subsidiaries, but the figure also includes payments from other foreign firms for li-

censes to use patented U.S. technologies or to manufacture
patented U.S. goods.

So some corporations — including many of the largest —
have not had as much concern about foreign competition as
might otherwise be expected. About one third of U.S.
imports, in fact, come from U.S.–owned operations abroad.
However, half of this total is accounted for by oil imports and
by imports of cars from U.S. automakers' plants in Canada.
Excluding these two special cases, about one sixth of U.S. imports come from foreign subsidiaries of U.S. companies.

There is something of an either-or choice about pursuing an
international business approach based on investment competition and pursuing an approach based on trade competition. The two approaches require different strategies about
the value of the dollar. Foreign investment is most profitable
when the value of the dollar is high relative to other currencies, because it becomes cheaper for U.S. businesses to
buy foreign factories. Trade, on the other hand, is most
successful when the value of the dollar is low, making U.S.
goods cheaper in foreign countries (see the final section of
this chapter).

Still, if five sixths of U.S. imports in most product lines come
from genuinely foreign firms, then being able to compete
effectively must be of some importance to many domestic
corporations. Why haven't they competed more effectively?
In some industries like shoes and textiles, where wages make
up by far the most important part of corporate costs, it may
be that low-wage competition from abroad was unbeatable.
Many firms have gone under, and others have moved overseas to join the competition.

But in more capital-intensive industries (those using more
machinery and fewer workers) wage competition alone does
not account for the United States losing its edge. In these industries, U.S. companies simply did not innovate as quickly
as foreign competitors, because in their view it was not profitable for them to do so.

The auto industry is a perfect example. When there was no

foreign competition worth worrying about and new car buyers had to swallow the models and prices decreed by Detroit, the automakers found it most profitable to put out an ever-growing number of big, luxury-oriented cars. They devoted their engineering effort to devising minor brand differences and annual model changes, so as to push up the price and also encourage consumers to change cars more often. They had no incentive to develop a small, low-cost, standardized car. As one GM executive put it, "Mini-cars mean mini-profits."

Even when VWs and later Datsuns and Toyotas flooded the U.S. market, Detroit's response was halfhearted. The Corvair, for instance, was the car that inspired Ralph Nader to write *Unsafe at Any Speed*, the 1966 book that established his reputation as a consumer advocate. Also, the first wave of compact cars got less compact every year. The later wave of subcompacts gave us the Vega, built on an assembly line designed to produce a car every thirty-six seconds — a line so fast that defects were inevitable. The second wave also produced the Pinto, the most dangerous car of the seventies. As a result, imports have developed a superior reputation, and their sales have continued to grow even though they now cost as much as or more than domestic cars.

In steel, too, U.S. companies fell behind in innovation — not in terms of the product in this case, but in the production process. The basic oxygen furnace, which has replaced the old open hearth furnace for turning iron into steel, was developed in Europe in the 1940s and introduced throughout Europe and Japan in the 1950s. But U.S. Steel, Bethlehem Steel, and Republic Steel — the top U.S. producers — did not adopt it until 1964, despite heavy investments in new mills (of the old type) in the 1950s. According to *Business Week*, in the fifties the American steel industry "added 40 million tons of the wrong type of capacity." The next major innovation, continuous casting, was adopted abroad in the early and mid-1960s, but barely had been adopted in the U.S. by 1970.

There are a variety of explanations for these delays.

Andrew Carnegie is supposed to have said, "It don't pay to be a pioneer"; perhaps the U.S. companies were waiting until foreign producers had paid the costs of testing and perfecting the new techniques. It's also been argued that U.S. firms are behind on many new techniques because so much of research-and-development funding in this country goes into strictly military applications. But underlying the failure to innovate must also have been a false sense of invulnerability that stemmed from the long period when the United States' lead over foreign competitors was so great.

Down into Deficits

The decline of U.S. economic power is reflected by the long-run decline in two key indicators: the balance of trade and the balance of payments. The balance of trade is a reflection of the international competition for sales. The balance of payments is a more complex measure, but it reflects a wider range of realities as well.

In the late 1940s and the 1950s the United States achieved a trade surplus of about $5 billion a year. That is, exports of U.S.–made goods brought in $5 billion more than was spent by U.S. businesses and consumers on imported foreign-made goods. Over half the surplus came from trade in capital goods (machinery used to produce other goods and services). Most of the rest came from the sale of manufactured goods. In food, petroleum, and other industrial materials and supplies (such as steel), the United States exported roughly the same amount that it imported.

In the early 1960s the trade surplus actually increased, as rising capital goods exports outweighed slight increases in consumer goods and petroleum imports. The surplus set a record in 1964 and then started its long slide down. By 1971, the trade balance showed a deficit (more imports than exports) for the first time in this century. The $2.3 billion deficit of 1971 was followed by a whopping $6.4 billion shortfall the following year.

The basic cause of the deficit was the rebuilt economies of Europe and Japan. But an important factor affecting its timing was the inflation brought about by the Vietnam War. During 1964–69, the prices of U.S. exports rose 10 percent more than the prices of German or Japanese exports, thus cutting the time it took foreign manufacturers to become competitive with U.S. companies.

The huge deficits that followed in later years (such as the $26.7 billion figure recorded for 1977), were swollen by the soaring price and quantity of imported oil. But in 1971–72 this was not yet a problem; the U.S. trade deficit with the oil-exporting countries was only about $500 million at the time — slightly *less* than it had been in 1960.

Table 5 shows the decline in the U.S. trade balance with other regions. From 1960 to 1972, the United States lost ground in trade with all the developed areas. It also lost ground in the three leading runaway-shop countries — Taiwan, Hong Kong, and South Korea — whose industry includes transplanted Japanese and American manufacturers as well as some locally owned firms.

What happened to trade after 1972 is included in the final section of this chapter. First, however, we need to look at the decline in the balance of payments — the measure of the flow of *money* into and out of the country for a variety of reasons, of which trade is only one.

When GM builds or buys a plant in Germany or Brazil, it takes money out of the country to do so. This outflow is usually more than balanced by the profits flowing back into the United States from such foreign operations. But the exercise of U.S. power in the postwar period has also involved a great deal of overseas spending by the federal government — for military bases and interventions, military aid, and economic aid — which brings no financial return. The purpose of much of this spending is to protect the worldwide investments of the U.S.-based multinationals. Along with the United States' privileged position as the world's dominant capitalist power came many of the international duties for-

Table 5

U.S. Balance of Trade, by Region, 1960, 1972, and 1977
(in billions of dollars)

	1960	1972	1977	Change from 1960-72	Change from 1972-77
World total	+5.9	−5.8	−26.7	−11.7	−20.9
West Germany	+0.4	−1.4	−1.2	−1.8	+0.2
Other West Europe	+2.6	+1.4	+7.6	−1.2	+6.2
Japan	+0.3	−4.1	−8.1	−4.4	−4.0
Other developed	+1.1	−2.0	−1.8	−3.1	+0.2
Oil countries	−0.6	−0.5	−22.6	+0.1	−22.1
Taiwan, Hong Kong and South Korea	+0.5	−1.4	−4.0	−1.9	−2.6
Other Third World	+1.1	+1.7	+1.5	+0.6	−0.2
Communist countries	+0.1	+0.5	+1.6	+0.4	+1.1

Note: Other developed countries are Canada, Australia, New Zealand, Israel, and South Africa. Oil countries are OPEC members plus Angola, Bahamas, Netherlands Antilles, Trinidad and Tobago.

Source: *Statistical Abstract*, 1975, 1978.

merly carried out by the European powers and Japan. Even in the late 1950s, when the United States still boasted a sizable *trade* surplus, these other outflows tended to create balance of *payments* deficits.

For most countries, such a deficit would quickly spell trouble. A negative balance of payments means a build-up of a given country's currency (British pounds, for instance) abroad. If foreigners find themselves accumulating more pounds than they have any use for, they will exchange them for other currencies. With more people trying to sell pounds than to buy them, the pound's exchange rate (that is, how many yen or marks or dollars it can be exchanged for) will drop. As Britain's position in the world declined, the value of the pound did indeed drop from $4.03 in the 1940s to $1.75 in 1977.

However, the unique position of the United States after World War II allowed it to create a charmed life for the dollar. When representatives of the Western powers gathered in 1944 at Bretton Woods, New Hampshire, to plan the finances of the postwar world, they agreed to set a high, fixed value for the dollar. U.S. business and government wanted a high value for the dollar; the more marks you could get for your dollar, the more factories or military bases you could buy in Germany. Also, the dollar became the standard against which the value of other currencies was measured. The dollar, in many ways, replaced gold as the medium of international exchange.

This system worked as long as the dollar was, indeed, "as good as gold." As long as the United States was the undisputed economic leader and U.S. goods were constantly in demand, dollars were in demand too. So the United States was able to run a balance of payments deficit without anyone getting too upset. Foreign governments and corporations were willing to hold large amounts of dollars because they knew that the dollar's value was stable.

But in the late 1960s the system began to come apart. The escalation of the Vietnam War increased government spending overseas at the same time as the trade position of private business deteriorated. Suddenly, the dollar was not as good as gold. Foreigners — and also U.S.-based multinationals — did not want to accumulate large amounts of dollars; they even began trying to get rid of them. In 1971, the dollar was devalued — that is, its official worth in terms of other currencies was lowered for the first time since Bretton Woods. There have been more devaluations since then, and, in fact, the leading capitalist powers have had to abandon the whole system of fixed exchange rates adopted at Bretton Woods. The value of the dollar now goes up and down freely — floats — as part of the trading and speculating in international money markets.

Although these pressures are pushing the value of the dollar down, it is still the major currency used in international trade, and many giant banks, corporations, and governments around the world hold tremendous amounts

of reserves in dollars. If the dollar were to plummet too far
or too fast, the result could be a financial panic leading to
chaos in the world economy. The holders of large dollar
reserves could find themselves bankrupt. No one would
know what dollar price to charge for their goods, since the
dollar's value might change drastically before payment was
made; world trade could slow to a crawl, throwing export-
oriented economies into recession or depression. Thus the
stability of the international capitalist system still rests on a
sound U.S. economy and a sound dollar.

One new dynamic in the world economy that is *not*
destabilizing the dollar is the growing wealth of OPEC
countries. Despite the U.S. trade deficit with OPEC, the
rising price of imported oil is not affecting the U.S. balance
of payments. The explanation is that the OPEC countries
have been investing a large part of their earnings in the
United States. All in all, between 1974 and 1977 the U.S.
balance of payments with OPEC countries showed a slight
surplus. Also, the necessity of spending large sums on imported oil is not a problem unique to the United States, but
one shared by Germany and Japan. The United States
actually possesses an advantage, in that it has significant
domestic supplies of oil whereas these major competitors
are totally dependent on imports. Thus their balance of exports versus imports is eroded at least as much as the U.S.
balance.

The United States Responds

In the 1970s American government and business have attempted to respond to the many-faceted problems of international economics. To some extent, they have succeeded
in halting the decline in the United States' international
position. But the weapons they must employ are the mirror
image of the weapons the Germans and Japanese made
use of to emerge as competitors in the first place. To the

extent that America can regain its edge in trade in the 1980s, it must do so at the expense of American workers and consumers.

In order to improve their competitive position, U.S. companies must somehow make their export goods cheaper. This is one of the chief reasons why they are concerned about uncontrolled inflation at home. If prices of U.S.-produced goods go up, these goods become harder to sell abroad. At the same time, U.S. firms would like to see foreign goods become more expensive, and therefore less attractive, to U.S. consumers.

One means of boosting exports and curtailing imports is — amazingly enough — devaluation of the dollar. The devaluations of 1971 and 1973, though bad for the purchasing power of U.S. business and for international stability, were good for the U.S. trade position. If a dollar becomes equal to fewer yen, then American goods will become cheaper for Japanese customers. By the same token, a yen becomes equal to more dollars, so Japanese products become more expensive here. This phenomenon is almost impossible for a normal human being to conceptualize in the abstract so, instead, try imagining that you are the owner of a Japanese car company:

When you sell cars in the United States, you receive your payment in dollars. But you have to pay your workers and materials suppliers at home in yen, since that is the local currency. So you have to turn those dollars into yen. If a dollar is worth 300 yen, you can sell a car for $3,000 in the United States and exchange that for 900,000 yen with which to meet your costs at home and retain a tidy profit. But if the value of the dollar sinks to 250 yen, that $3,000 car brings you only 750,000 yen; the other 150,000 yen that you used to make on each U.S. sale has vanished into thin air. The only way to maintain your take of 900,000 yen per car is to raise the U.S. price to $3,600. Since the value of the dollar actually dropped from 293 yen at the end of 1976 to only 195 yen at the end of 1978, the cause of the soaring price of Japanese cars in U.S. showrooms is easy to see.

By this process of cheapening U.S. exports while making imports more expensive, the dollar devaluations of 1971 and 1973 succeeded in bringing the U.S. trade balance to a slight surplus in 1973. When the trade deficit with Europe and Japan was rising in 1978, the plummeting dollar again helped to reverse the trend. But at times like these, U.S. officials come under intense pressure from multinational corporations, banks, and foreign governments, who fear for the value of their dollar reserves and also fear the coming of a financial panic. In October 1978, *Business Week* reported "a constant barrage of criticism of U.S. policy by European and Japanese officials." The president of West German's central bank stated that it was "absolutely necessary" for the United States to slow down its economy so as to stop "sucking in" imports (which lead to devaluation). "For the first time in seven years," the magazine reported, "U.S. policymakers are now giving the state of the dollar almost equal priority with domestic considerations." The following month the administration came forward with a program to stabilize the dollar. "A failure to act would have been injurious to the U.S. and the world economy," stated Treasury Secretary Blumenthal. "The fall of the dollar must and will end."

A dangerous side effect of devaluation is that it fuels inflation at home. Not only does the price of a Datsun go up, but Ford and GM can raise the prices of their compacts to nearly the same level. The inflation gradually spreads throughout the whole economy. Once again U.S. exports become more expensive.

Devaluation also adds to inflation through its effect on oil prices. OPEC prices, regardless of who is buying the oil, are set in terms of dollars. When the value of the dollar drops, OPEC countries will raise oil prices just to stay even. The real (discounted for inflation) price of crude oil actually dropped between 1974 and 1978, providing one impetus for the 1979 round of increases.

Another means of limiting imports is through tariffs and quotas. But protectionism is a two-way street. Foreign countries can respond in kind and close off their markets to U.S. exports. A major international trade war could result, causing drops in production and even depressions world-wide. Though some U.S. industries (such as steel, textiles, and shoes) have been clamoring for protectionist poli-cies, the government and most business interests are more interested in pushing for a lowering of trade barriers by all sides.

The 1973 to 1979 Tokyo Round (of international trade negotiations) — once its provisions are ratified by the legis-latures of the nations involved — will have exactly that effect of lowering trade barriers. The United States' compe-titors — particularly Japan — agreed to lower their barriers the fastest. This slight victory for American business reflects the European fear of a catastrophic trade war or dollar col-lapse which could happen if the United States' position drops too fast. U.S. business now gains concessions, it appears, by playing chicken rather than Monopoly.

As far as the job picture here is concerned, a Congres-sional Budget Office study of the Tokyo Round estimated that "the net change in employment will probably be very small." That is, the jobs created in the industries that can compete most successfully will be balanced by the jobs lost in the weaker industries. But the new jobs are for different kinds of workers, in different parts of the country, than the old jobs that will be destroyed. New computer jobs in Massachusetts and California are little comfort to unem-ployed steelworkers in Ohio or textile workers in North Carolina.

The remaining weapon in the trade-arsenal is recession. When the Carter Administration was under pressure in late 1978 to do something about the falling dollar, it hiked in-terest rates. One immediate goal was to attract some for-eign investment funds, since investors could earn higher interest on bonds and other securities here than abroad. But the long-term purpose was to push the economy in the direction of recession. The boost in interest rates was accompanied by other measures to tighten monetary policy and by declarations about holding the line on federal spending as well. The Treasury Department admitted to lowering its estimation of "what is an appropriate level of growth for this economy." "For once they got it right," applauded an international economist at Morgan Guaranty Trust. "They have finally bitten the bullet."

It's not surprising that a move toward recession should restore confidence in the dollar. The 1974–75 recession was the best thing that happened to U.S. trade in the 1970s. The surplus with non-OPEC countries that began with the dollar devaluations of 1971 and 1973 continued upward to a peak of more than $30 billion in 1975. As incomes fell in the United States, Americans could afford fewer imports, while other countries could still buy U.S. exports. (When the recession reached the other capitalist countries and recovery began at home, however, the effect was reversed.)

Recessions are also helpful to trade because they hold down wages, making it easier for corporations to keep costs down and thus to compete more effectively. On the other hand, a long period of economic growth and rising wages tends to hurt the balance of trade. So, if it is trying to protect the balance of trade, the government is likely to cause or allow more frequent recessions. In Britain, where trade problems have been more severe for much longer than in the United States, the result has become known as the "stop-go" economic policy.

Who will gain and who will lose in the coming years is anybody's guess. Between 1972 and 1977 (see Table 5) the U.S. sharply improved its trade balance with the weaker countries of Western Europe, improved slightly with respect to Germany, and continued to fall behind Japan. The dollar drop in 1978 brought more improvement. European and Japanese firms are responding to devaluation by building plants here, mostly in low-wage regions. In the 1980s, Japanese companies may face higher labor costs and more social legislation and environmental costs at home as the realities of rapid development finally catch up with them. Germany, on the other hand, is making a bid for increased dominance in Europe. And multinational corporations based in all the developed countries will continue to move parts of their operations to the Third World

Conflicts over world economic dominance used to be resolved by war. Both world wars have brought major socialist revolutions in their wake, however, and the major powers are now united in a single anti-communist military alliance. An economic war, with each nation or group of nations raising higher and higher import barriers, is possible, though the major powers seem to recognize the common danger. Probably, the 1980s will bring more of what we've seen in the 1970s: a combination of multinationalization and competition among the corporations of the developed countries, with attempts to transfer the costs to their own people through recession, currency manipulation, plant shutdowns, and patriotic appeals for wage restraint and higher productivity. It's a type of economic cold war from which none of us have very much to gain.

8.
CONCLUSION: IS THERE AN ALTERNATIVE?

Since 1945, the real U.S. Gross National Product per person has doubled. That is, the value of the nation's output of goods and services, corrected for inflation, has risen twice as fast as the population. The phenomenal ability of American capitalism to produce and produce and produce has been taken as evidence of its efficiency, its rationality, its ability to meet the needs of the nation.

But what do such statistical reflections of economic growth really tell us beyond the tremendous volume of products exchanged every year? Does a bigger and better GNP mean a better life? What does GNP tell us about the welfare of U.S. citizens?

Not much. To begin with, the aggregate GNP figures tell us nothing about the usefulness of what is produced. GNP includes everything sold in the economy — and everything provided by the government — no matter how worthless or harmful it may be. Bombs, cigarettes, bubblegum; pop rocks, and pet rocks; violent television, FBI surveillance, country club memberships, and *Time* magazine; nuclear reactors, presidential elections, electric carving knives, and fluorocarbon hairsprays; polyvinyl chloride and forced sterilization — they're all lumped right in there with milk, bread, housing construction, and health services.

What's more, GNP numbers don't tell us much about the distribution of the so-called wealth of our nation. A $200 evening for two in a fancy restaurant enters into GNP equally with the $200 grocery basket that must feed a family of four for two weeks. The GNP doesn't tell us what jobs are like for those working at them or how jobs are affected by productivity measures that boost the GNP. As the gap between what our economy produces and what we actually need continues to widen, GNP keeps right on going.

These failings in the GNP figure are no mere statistical quirks. The economic system that they reflect is based above all on *how much* can be profitably sold, to the exclusion of *what* is produced, *for whom,* and *how.* We've talked over and over again about how the pursuit of profits is the source of many specific problems, about business as a self-interested, antisocial force. But the problem is not a simple one of profits being too high, of business being too greedy — to be solved by statutory profit controls or a redistribution of profits through taxation.

The problem, in essence, is not one of how much money goes to profits, but it is that the quest for profits dictates the uses of our natural and human resources. The "put in the least to get back the most" logic of the profit and market systems permeates every facet of our society. From corporate board rooms and the Oval Office to our workplaces, classrooms, and living rooms, the "minimize costs, maximize returns" reasoning determines both our social and individual priorities.

No society can afford to give all the fruits of labor back to the individual producers. Some share of what's made and exchanged must be set aside for new investments in the research, machinery, or materials that make it possible to produce more and different goods and services. In a capitalist economy — as corporate message advertisers such as Mobil and Chase Manhattan never tire of telling us — that set-aside share is profits. But what is unique to capitalism — something neglected in those corporate public relations ads — is that the accumulation of profits is the sole motivating force behind production; that the decisions about what to do with these profits are made solely by the owners of the private businesses, for the purpose of reinvesting to accumulate even more profits.

Though we have repeatedly pointed an accusing finger at business and employers, it is not a problem of demonic executives or secret conspiracies. Suppose, for example, that the chairman of the board of the mythical firm Pan-Universal General Enterprises is captured and held prisoner for nearly a year by a group of revolutionaries in the Philippines to protest Pan-Universal's presence on the islands. The chairman's eleven-month ordeal gives him a lot of time to reflect on what his captors are saying, and he vows to turn Pan-Universal into a model of social responsibility. Once back in the executive saddle, he donates the firm's Philippine factories to the workers there, closes its South African gold mines, and institutes day-care services and maternity and paternity leave for employees of the company's nursing home chain. Finally, he instructs the star of the corporate family — the beverage container division — to produce only reusable bottles.

As a result of these unusual corporate policies, Pan-Universal's costs rise and its sales fall. There aren't enough profits to finance the new slum-rehabilitation division, and the banks are unwilling to lend to the company because they doubt that the projected rent levels will allow Pan-Universal to pay the going rate of interest. The value of the company's once-blue-chip stock plummets, and the stockholders are desperate to unload. In the end, Pan-Universal falls victim to a takeover by Consolidated Ultrabig. The chairman is deemed eccentric and replaced by a more "responsible" executive. He spends the rest of his days at one of the firm's nursing homes, pondering the fate of his seemingly reasonable plan.

In a sense, the chairman's new corporate priorities *were* eccentric. While the free enterprise system prides itself on being a system that offers a high degree of personal choice, those choices are ironically limited by the system itself. As the options open to Pan-Universal were limited, so too are all of our options as workers and consumers. We may appear to have many options, because we have been taught to believe that the choices between brands of cigarettes and toilet paper are indeed choices. We are free to choose between a dull, aggravating salesclerk job and one in a dangerous, noisy factory. Or, if we are blessed with a' higher-class position, perhaps we can choose between a job in business that creates social problems and one in social work or education that fails to solve them.

Even the options that confront us as a society are no-win ones. Can we choose higher wages, more labor-saving machinery, *and* secure, meaningful work for all? Can we control what policies our elected officials — Democratic or Republican — will make? Can we choose *neither* inflation nor recession? Can we choose to eliminate sex roles, or only to extend them so that those who make the beds for free at home make them for wages in the hospitals as well? Can we choose what kind of energy alternatives we care to explore, what medical research we'd like to pursue? It may be true that no one tells a company what to make or how to make it or an individual where to work or what to buy, but real choices are beyond our control.

The logic of the system thus limits what we as a society can achieve. It also limits what we as individuals can or are likely to believe. Not only businesspeople, but all of us, have become accustomed to putting our own interests first. The logic of the system rewards us for being competitive rather than cooperative, for ignoring social consequences rather than being conscious of them.

Look at the automobile. It's a commonplace observation by now that the United States is overly dependent on the private automobile. If you can afford one, getting by without a car is a possibility only if you live and work in the central city and have no desire, or opportunity, to leave it. Even then, managing to work, run errands, and take in any entertainment using public transportation is quite a chore. According to the most recent census data, in 1974 84 percent of all households owned one or more private automobiles. This situation is not a result of personal choice. It is the result of government subsidization of the auto and oil industries by funding highway construction rather than mass transit. It is also the result of the purposeful destruction of private electric trolley systems in forty-five cities between 1936 and 1949 by General Motors, Standard Oil of California, and Firestone Tire. (As detailed in an amazing report issued by the Senate Anti-trust Subcommittee in 1974, these firms created a holding company to buy trolley systems, rip up miles of tracks, replace the trolleys with diesel buses, and then resell the systems. Buses created less interference with car traffic and more sales for GM, Standard, and Firestone, but they made for more pollution and less efficient and attractive mass transit.)

Within the logic of capitalism, the decision to favor private cars over public transportation is a rational one for businesses, and, therefore, becomes one for individuals as well. The production of the maximum number of vehicles and consumption of the maximum amount of fuel makes for the maximum accumulation of profit. The waste, pollution, and aggravation — which ranges from the occasional energy-crunch-imposed gasoline line to the daily and all too familiar traffic jam — involved in a car-commuting society do not show up on corporate balance sheets. The personal expenditures required for repairs, insurance, and loan payments are simply income for other businesses. So two generations of Americans have grown up in a world that revolves around the private car, and cars have crept into our minds, not merely as necessities, but also as symbols of status, success, and even freedom. The opportunity to jump into our own gas-guzzling, polluting, accident-prone vehicle and go where we want is something that most of us prize highly. And why shouldn't we? Given the lack of a systematic alternative, what good would it do the air, the society, or our own sanity if, on any particular occasion when we did have a choice, we stayed home?

This doesn't mean that there's nothing we can do — now — to change many things in our present system. We are *not* powerless. Many forms of protection we've discussed throughout the book — from workplace safety regulations, unions, and affirmative action to social services, partial price controls, and unemployment compensation — exist because people have organized themselves and demanded these protections.

Every day, in small ways, tenants stand up to landlords; employees stand up to employers; farmworkers, consumers, and small farmers stand up to agribusiness. This occurs not only individually but collectively — through tenants' unions, workplace women's caucuses, and food and farming cooperatives. Applying political pressure brings about government services such as publicly funded day care and emergency winter fuel supplies. It is possible, too, to create small independent organizations that are not run for profit, that disseminate information and help people in the most human and honest way possible; alternative schools are an outstanding example (see How to Survive at the back of the book for the names of specific groups to contact).

Such organizations and programs do not fall from the sky. The active and increasingly powerful anti-nuclear power groups, for instance, did not come ready-formed when a power company put up its first reactor. Rather, they sprang up when people who lived near nuclear power plants discovered the potential hazards and were angry enough to try to stop construction, shut down plants, or spread the word to others who may be faced with similar plants in their own backyards. As a result, the dangers have been brought to the attention of the country, regulations have been toughened, and many proposed plants have been held up long enough that the utilities may have to abandon them.

Working together, beating the system here and there, stopping a nuclear power plant all help us in the short-run, aid us in changing our viewpoints and prejudices, give us

the sense that we can and have to do something in order
to live the way we feel is safe, healthy, and fulfilling. But
such actions and movements are not enough. Beating the
system does not change it, and the same problems continue to confound us. To really change the conditions under
which we live, we can't stop here.

Could society really be different? Neither would we have
written this book, nor would the *Dollars & Sense* collective
publish a magazine, if it weren't for our belief that the capitalist system can be replaced by something better. We believe that a socialist society is neither a utopian dream nor
an inevitably repressive attempt to tinker with the facts of
economic life and human nature. Rather, it is a logical exit
from the maze of limited opportunities we have just
described.

Why socialism? Socialism offers the possibility of society's
members rationally balancing various needs, whereas capitalism offers nothing but the pursuit of private accumulation
through thoughtless and antisocial competition. A socialist
system requires *public ownership* AND *control* over the
productive facilities of the economy, over the working
conditions, over how the wealth that results from production will be reinvested and distributed. The relative usefulness of different types of investments could be a subject of
practical and public concern, with consideration given to
their effect on the whole society. If the fulfillment of public
needs replaces the accumulation of private profit as the
key economic priority, personal participation in social
decision making becomes a possibility, opening up many
other avenues in all facets of life.

Look at transportation again. In a socialist society, the
social costs of dependence on the personal automobile
could figure in the economic decisions. The types of mass
transportation and the forms of single-vehicle transportation
could emerge from a decision-making process that
weighed the needs of urban, suburban, and rural residents;
the quality of the air; the availability of resources. Once the

costs involved in large scale commuting were considered as part of the cost of production, it would become logical to provide people with work closer to their homes as well.

Take, for instance, the connection between cars and houses. In our present economy, a drop in auto production doesn't lead to more housing construction; on the contrary, the opposite is true. Auto workers and workers in related industries are laid off and therefore can't buy houses, so housing construction slows down. Yet in an economy that rationally planned and allocated its resources, the human and physical resources saved by a lower automobile output could instead be devoted to building homes. Housing would not be a commodity produced only when it could be sold at a profit, but a necessity to be produced in whatever quantity and quality the society could afford.

We are taught to think of ideals like these as the visions of dreamers, unpragmatic, alien to the practical spirit of America. Precisely because our society and economy are so large, so chaotic, so removed from our control, it is very difficult to believe that we have the intelligence and skill to reorder them. The idea that a simple change in ownership would make the difference seems particularly dubious.

Socialism, though, signifies much more than a simple change in ownership. It's true that establishing a socialist society requires a decisive act — the taking of the society's resources from the hands of private owners. But that event is only the beginning of an ongoing process of constructing true public control.

It is important to make this distinction between ownership and control. In the United States today, there are numerous experiments with employee-owned companies. Yet the employee ownership of these individual workplaces does not mean that the employee-owners can control what goes on in the economy as a whole, how profit-run businesses will price or allocate their raw materials; what the demand for their products will be. Further, employee ownership of a company does not automatically ensure democratic decision making among all the owners.

In a northern corner of Vermont, the Vermont Asbestos Group (VAG) mine is one such worker-owned company, where ownership proved to be one thing and workplace democracy yet another. It is an example familiar to us, since we visited with workers there in 1975 and again in 1978. The asbestos operation was bought in 1975 from the international conglomerate GAF, which had formerly run it; employees and local residents paid $50 per share to become the mine's new owners. The company was run by a board of directors made up of seven production workers, seven other employees who had been either foremen or middle managers under the previous owner, and one outside representative. The board was to supervise the running of the operation much like any other company's board, though major decisions were subject to a shareholders' vote.

This small mine (employing 175 people), in its first year, went on to financial success; VAG's stock jumped from the near-bankruptcy price of $50 a share at which employees and residents bought it, to $2,000 a share by the spring of 1978. But VAG was lucky; the larger, conventional asbestos industry took a turn for the worse the very year the mine's ownership changed hands. Several big asbestos mines in Canada — this country's largest source of the raw material — were shut down by strikes and natural disasters. While demand continued to grow, VAG prospered and the new owners were able to accomplish some things. They were able to keep the mine open and preserve their jobs — the very reason employee ownership was originally proposed. They made government-mandated engineering changes to limit pollution and protect employee health and safety, which cost $1.3 million — something the old owners found too expensive. And they gave a somewhat larger share of the wealth produced by the operation to the production workers, through an improved union contract and benefits of stock ownership.

By 1977, the limits of individual employee-owned companies began to surface. The company's earnings, though still totaling $900,000, were declining as the asbestos market tightened. But more important, it became apparent that most workers at VAG had gained very little control over the operation. Though a few production workers were elected to the board of directors, it remained dominated by management employees who had more expertise or experience in running a company. And no new decision-making structures that would lead to more democratic planning of the company's direction were introduced. Until 1977, this wasn't exactly a noticeable problem at VAG; shareholders' lack of leverage was mostly limited to scattered expressions of dissatisfaction. The decline in earnings worried employees, but what turned the dissatisfaction and disunity into widespread outrage was the July 1977 decision of the board to develop a wallboard subsidiary with full VAG financing — when the shareholders' vote had mandated that VAG should shoulder only 50 percent of the cost. As a result, many workers became disillusioned with the concept of employee ownership; by the spring of 1978, many had sold their shares to outside investors. As one asbestos-bagging machine operator put it: "I sold my shares because I was fed up. I figured it might be a way to be through with haggling."

The same process can occur with nationalized industries. To create socialism requires not just taking over the industries, but creating forms by which they are publicly controlled. This involves not just the creation of democratic structures that look good on paper, but the creation of a consciousness in which we become accustomed to thinking of ourselves as part of something larger — as part of society as a whole. Through such a broader view of life, goals, and priorities, people become capable of playing a truly active part in the running of society.

This is a tremendous task, considering the very private and competitive outlook we inherit from a capitalist economy. The change in consciousness cannot spring into being at the time of the decisive political event. It must begin to emerge during the social struggles that will have to be waged to seize the ownership of society's resources, struggles that bring people together and show them that things can and should be different.

There are plenty of examples of such changes in consciousness in our own history, which changed the outlook and sense of power of the many who were involved. The unionization struggles of the Industrial Workers of the World in the opening decades of the century and the Congress of Industrial Organizations in the 1930s and 1940s developed among millions of people a sense of the meaning of collective action and the right of working people to a say about the conditions in which they work. The civil rights and black power movements involved not only an atmosphere of close solidarity among participants, but a transformation of the self-image of black Americans. The women's liberation movement has meant the same for millions of women. And the movement against the Vietnam War represented a decision by countless citizens that they, not those whose job it was to plan foreign policy, knew what was best for the country. We are not discussing here a strategy or a prediction about how future mass movements for socialism will come about. But we think it is evident that these movements will bring with them ever greater changes in the self-image and social outlook of participants.

Socialism is hardly an ideal that we dreamed up in some vacant corner of our brains. The striving for socialism by small clubs, utopian communities, political parties, and even governments has more than a century of history to its credit (and sometimes discredit). Do existing societies that describe themselves as socialist offer any evidence that our vision can become a reality?

To begin with, we must stress a point of definition that

may seem elementary or pedantic, but one that has been so thoroughly obscured by the media and educational system in this country that very few people actually understand it. A recent questionnaire designed to test U.S. high school students' knowledge of social studies stated that the Soviet Union has a communist system and Sweden has a socialist one, and asked what type the United States has. But both of those statements are wrong. Sweden does not describe itself as a socialist country; more important, the bulk of its industry remains privately owned. Nor is the Soviet Union, by its own or any other meaningful definition, a communist society.

None of the countries today ruled by communist parties refer to their societies as communist. Communism, in Marxist theory, refers to a final stage of development in which classes, hierarchies, the state, money, material inequalities, and other characteristics of a class society have been entirely eliminated, replaced by voluntary organization and a maximum level of consciousness of the effects of one's actions on others. It is an ideal toward which energies should be directed, one that current structures and methods should promote but cannot be expected to live up to.

Socialism is a long transitional stage characterized by public ownership of the means of production; guarantees of employment and basic products and services to all citizens; an end to discrimination on the basis of sex or race; just rewards for work; and the growth of democratic forms and collective consciousness. Though it eliminates the coercive power of private business in the workplace and the marketplace, it does not eliminate all forms of coercion.

The attempts to put this theory into practice have all occurred in societies that were economically underdeveloped and threatened by powerful capitalist countries. We believe that this circumstance has been a major cause of their employing more coercion and less democracy than we would like to see. In any event, we do not hold any of them up as a model of what we mean by socialism in the United States.

Still, we think that these societies, in varying degrees, have demonstrated that the choices offered by capitalism can be significantly broadened by an alternative system. The process with which we are most familiar is the one that has unfolded over the past twenty years in Cuba. We've had the opportunity to work and travel there on two occasions a decade apart, and we've found it to be an inspiring example of the types of changes that are possible.

It is important to remember that in 1959 Cuba was at a much less developed stage of material wealth and technology than our own country — choosing the socialist path, in fact, because domination by U.S. business prevented the balanced development of its economy. It is also a country of 10 million people rather than 200 million. Thus the specific problems to be solved have been quite different from those facing a large industrialized country like the United States; the specific solutions made possible by a socialist alternative in the United States would also be quite different. It's also significant, in evaluating the successes and limitations of socialism in Cuba, that the new government had to face a total economic embargo imposed by the United States, which had been Cuba's largest trading partner. Economic and military aid from the Soviet Union has made it possible for Cuba to survive, though it has imposed some political constraints as well.

So we are not presenting Cuba as model for the United States, but as an example of the types of changes that a shift from capitalism to socialism can bring. Specifically, the Cuban revolution has involved many more people in political and economic decision making than was possible before; it has provided economic security and basic human services; it has given most Cubans more personal choices than they had under capitalism; and it has brought about wide-ranging changes in personal consciousness.

Decision making

Public ownership in Cuba has brought a great deal of public control, though the control is far from total. The distribution of much of the new housing is decided by discussion and voting in workplace assemblies, according to individual worker's needs and their contribution to production. Not only the wage scales but also the factory output quotas are negotiated between the unions and the government and must be approved by vote of the workers. A new family code, which includes the provision that housework must be shared by husband and wife, was proposed by the Cuban Women's Federation (a mass organization that all women may join) and discussed and voted on in local assemblies around the country. In most of these cases, the initiatives still come from above, but there are many channels of communication in both directions.

Economic planning issues — such as the balance between exports and domestic consumption of consumer goods or building materials — are approved by vote of various types of elected delegates, but they are not really subject to effective control at the base. What has changed, however, is that these decisions are the subject of detailed public discussion and must be justified in terms of their relation to the overall plan. The hours-long speeches by Fidel Castro described in the U.S. press are usually devoted to straightforward discussion of just such issues.

Decisions once made in the secrecy of sugar company headquarters in New York or exclusive private clubs in Havana are now made openly. This does not merely reflect good faith on the part of high officials; it reflects the reality that in a society where jobs and income are assured, workers will not produce without a larger reason.

Economic Security

There are no recessions, and the prices of necessities are low and stable. The annual "dead season" after the sugar harvest once condemned hundreds of thousands of workers to joblessness and poverty each year; now employment is a right guaranteed by the state. No one can be laid off or even fired. The most severe penalty — applied only by an elected workers' committee — is to be transferred to another workplace.

The mechanization of agricultural work, far from creating a mass of landless slum-dwellers as it does elsewhere in Latin America, eliminates some of the country's most backbreaking work, while opening up new job and study opportunities. The movement of sugar cane cutters from the cane fields to schools, new agricultural projects, and more highly skilled jobs actually began well before effective mechanization, and volunteer delegations of workers from other industries were used to fill the gap.

Services

In the capitalist period, professional health care was available only to those who could afford it, which in practice meant only those who lived in the cities. Half the doctors, seeing their privileged positions threatened, fled at the time of the revolution. Nonetheless, expanded educational opportunity has succeeded in more than replacing them, and the state-run health care system has created a network of quality clinics (whose physicians also make regular home visits) and hospitals throughout the country. Preventive inoculation programs carried out through grass-root neighborhood organizations have succeeded in eliminating the communicable diseases that ravage much of Latin America.

Transportation is based on an extensive network of urban, inter-urban, rural, and factory buses and a rebuilt national railroad. Private cars from the prerevolutionary period remain, but new cars are imported only for public uses and for sale to individuals whose jobs require them. The bus system in the capital city of Havana, however, is seriously overloaded. Government policy has always been to devote the maximum possible resources to the countryside, which was neglected under capitalism. Development plans call for restricting the growth of the capital while developing small cities in the interior.

Personal choice

The multiple choices of a consumer society are absent in Cuba. There are no different brands of beer; there is only beer, in unmarked returnable bottles. Many necessities are rationed to ensure equal distribution. Durable goods in short supply — not only houses, but refrigerators and televisions — are often distributed through the workplace. But the appearance of more choice in the capitalist period is an illusion; though there was no formal rationing through coupons or ration books, prices were in a sense a form of rationing that limited what consumers could buy. Before the revolution, most Cubans' incomes limited them to quantities of food and consumer goods far smaller than what they can purchase today under rationing. Housing construction — other than of the luxury variety — was almost nonexistent, and most consumer goods were luxury items available only as imports from the United States.

Job choices have been immensely broadened. One can no longer set up in business as an interior decorator for the rich (the former profession of a Cuban exile neighbor of ours), but there are no longer 10,000 teachers condemned to unemployment by the lack of comprehensive and quality schools. Women are still denied entrance to certain jobs in heavy industry, but the provisions of day care and equal education as well as the legal rejection of the notion that women must do the housework have made most jobs much more accessible to women than they were in the past. A country in which the private ballet societies routinely denied entrance to blacks is now internationally recognized for its public ballet company that encompasses dancers of all shades.

Consciousness

There is no way to prove with facts and numbers the

existence of a process of changing consciousness, whether
the numbers are of blood donors or volunteer workers or
boys growing up doing housework. Perhaps the most striking
"fact" would be the remark of an older Cuban man — a truck-
driver probably in his fifties — whom we met last year in a
provincial capital. He had been quiet during much of our visit
to his family's apartment, while his wife (an elected leader in
her workplace) had answered our questions about the
changes in the society. But after he put on his dress clothes
and began with some formality to show us around the neighborhood, we chanced to mention that people in the United
States are usually afraid of the idea of socialism, and to ask
how his opinions had changed with the change in social
systems.

"It's a very complex thing," he replied. "Very hard for you
to understand. The two systems are totally opposite. They
look at the world in two opposite ways, and of the two, socialism is much more just. But I cannot truly call myself a socialist.
I am a sympathizer of socialism, because it is a more just
system. But I come from the former time. Those who are
growing up in the new way, they can really think in the new
way."

We think those examples, though sketchy, are instructive.
Anyone who has traveled elsewhere in Latin America will
find them particularly so. We hope, however, that the wealth
and power of the United States would make possible many
more experiments with democratization of the workplace,
decentralization of decision-making, new and more humane
uses of technology, and reliance on initiatives from below —
experiments that have not appeared in a society like Cuba,
still struggling to get out of underdevelopment and to resist
economic blockade and political subversion from the north.

What we can achieve in our own society will depend on
many things — on international events beyond our control;
on our skill at devising immediate goals, strategies, and ways
of talking and acting that make it possible to build powerful

broad-based movements; on mistakes and divisions in the dominant class. But it also depends on grounding our hopes in a thorough understanding of realities. We believe that an honest look at our society reveals that its problems are not solvable within the present framework. Those who believe in tinkering with the capitalist system — a reform here, an adjustment there, soon we'll get it right — are the dreamers. Those who believe that we can and must replace the system with a better one are the realists.

GLOSSARY OF COMMONLY USED TERMS

Accumulation — This is used to describe the process of firms successfully making money for their owners — not because those people need it to buy more goods, but rather because they need it if they're going to expand their businesses in order to make more money. This drive to accumulate is the main motivation of firms in a capitalist society.

Balance of Payments — Payments are made between the United States and other countries for purposes other than trade. For example, a U.S. firm may buy a factory abroad: this payment involves money going out of the United States. At the same time, companies are returning profits obtained abroad to the United States: these payments involve money coming in. Other types of payments include: U.S. government military purchases abroad (money going out) and purchases of U.S. stocks and bonds by foreigners (money coming in).

The total of all payments coming into the country in a particular time period minus the payments going out is the balance of payments. It is an overall measure of whether U.S. interests (firms, government, individuals) are taking in more than they are paying out. If more is coming in than going out, it is a *balance of payments surplus;* if more is going out than coming in, it is a *balance of payments deficit.*

The United States had a balance of payments deficit, even though it had a balance of trade surplus, throughout the late 1950s and the 1960s.

Balance of Trade — The value of all U.S.–produced goods sold abroad (exports) minus the value of all foreign-made goods sold in the United States (imports) is the balance of trade. If the balance of trade is positive, the country has a *trade surplus* (more money is coming in to pay for exports than is going out to pay for imports). If the balance is negative, that is, if imports exceed exports, the country has a *trade deficit* (more money is going out to pay for imports than is coming in to pay for exports).

Capital — This term has two very different meanings: (1) Sometimes capital is used to mean manufactured physical objects — machines, equipment, buildings — that are used in the production process, or money available to buy these objects. (2) In Marxist economics capital means more than just money or machines. It is the near monopoly over money and machinery by a small group of people (capitalists) who are able to hire other people to work for them, in order to make more money. Capital is thus a social relationship; most people have to work for someone else in order to survive.

Capital in the first sense — physical objects — is necessary for production in every economic system. However, capital in the second sense — the ability of the owners of those physical objects (means of production) to hire others to work for them — is unique to capitalism.

Capitalism — Capitalism is an economic system based on a wage-labor market and private ownership of the means of production.

In capitalism, most people have to work for someone else for wages if they are going to survive. Thus company owners can ensure themselves of the use of other people's labor to increase their own wealth.

Private ownership means not simply that people own personal property (which can be true in many economic systems), but that they can also own and control the use of productive objects — machinery, tools, buildings, and equipment — that other people worked to create.

Cartel — A group of firms or countries that jointly decides on prices and output. By coordinating actions, they can be certain not to disturb each other's profits. Cartels have existed for well over a century. The well-known Organization of Petroleum Exporting Countries is now using a tactic that large and powerful firms (including the oil companies) have used for generations.

Class — A class, in Marxist economics, consists of people who have the same role in the process of production. The two basic classes under capitalism are the capitalist, or ruling, class — those who own and control business — and the working class — who because they lack that control have to sell their labor for wages.

The Marxist use of the word *class* is different from that promoted by many sociologists, who use the term *class* to refer to level of income rather than relationship to the process of production.

Concentration — This is a measure of the control firms wield over a market; it tells what fraction of sales are controlled by the largest firms. The more concentrated a market, the more control individual firms exert over the level of profits and prices.

Consumer Price Index — See *Inflation*.

Deficit Spending — The government spends a huge amount of money on war, highways, unemployment checks, education, and many other things. When the government spends more than it collects in taxes, it is called "running a deficit." Deficit spending must be financed by borrowing. The U.S. government currently spends more than 10 percent of its budget on interest payments on the national debt, which has resulted from its past deficit spending.

Devaluation and Revaluation — The price of a currency is determined by the relative supply and demand for that currency. For example, the exchange rate of the dollar for yen will tend to fall if the demand for dollars by the Japanese is lessening. The demand for dollars might fall if, for example, there were declining sales of U.S. goods in Japan (declining U.S. exports), for then the Japanese would have less need for dollars.

Also, the exchange rate of dollars for yen will tend to fall if the supply of dollars being offered for yen rises, as when U.S. customers buy a lot of Japanese imports. (Other international payments also affect the supply for dollars relative to yen: the exchange rate does not depend solely on trade.)

When the exchange rate of one currency in terms of another currency falls, the first currency has been *devalued* in terms of the second, and the second has been *revalued* in terms of the first.

Fiscal Policy — See *Stimulation*.

Fixed Exchange Rates — Before 1971, the major trading partners of the United States tried to maintain constant or fixed exchange rates between each of their currencies and the dollar. If the exchange rate of pounds for dollars, for instance, began to fall, the

Bank of England would exchange dollars for pounds (borrowing dollars to do so if necessary) to maintain demand for, and hence the exchange rate of, the pound. However, this could counteract only short-run changes in the value of a currency. If the forces pushing down the value of the pound were lasting, the British government would have to declare a new, lower exchange rate between the dollar and the pound.

Floating Exchange Rates — The system of fixed exchange rates was abandoned by the United States and its principal trading partners in 1971. Major changes in the international economy — especially the instability of the U.S. economy and the consequent instability of the dollar — were making the old system unworkable. (Many countries with smaller, more dependent economies still attempt to maintain a fixed relation between their currencies and that of one of the major nations, like Mexico with the United States or Denmark with West Germany).

Now, if the pound starts to decline in value relative to the dollar, the British government does not try to stop it as before. The new system is one of floating exchange rates and involves day-to-day changes in the relative values of currencies. Governments, however, have not totally abandoned efforts to affect the values of their currencies and sometimes take what they deem "necessary actions." Consequently, the current system is sometimes called a "dirty float."

Gross National Product — The Gross National Product (GNP) is the total dollar value of all the goods and services produced for sale by U.S. firms. GNP is the total output of U.S. firms both at home and abroad. However, it is not a measure of all the useful and necessary things people do; the unpaid work that women do in the household is not included in the calculation, whereas many forms of useless production are.

Imperialism — This term stands for a whole network of methods of control (economic, political, military, and cultural) that the dominant groups in one country use to subjugate and exploit people in other countries. The power of the United States, Japanese, and Western European governments and corporations in numerous areas of the world has been and still is the major cause of underdevelopment.

Inflation — Inflation means simply that the price of nearly everything is going up. You may keep track of inflation by watching your bank balance decline, but the Labor Department's monthly Consumer Price Index (CPI) is the government's official measure of what's happening to prices.

Tne CPI is an index of the cost of the contents of a "market basket" of consumer items — a basket big and versatile enough to hold houses, used cars, restaurant meals, electricity, repairs, and a host of other items, necessary and luxurious, tangible and intangible. Each item is supposed to be represented in proportion to how much of our incomes we spend on it. The figure usually cited as the rate of inflation is the rate at which the CPI rises.

Leading Indicators — Since reading the future in the stars is hardly an appropriate way for economists to make predictions, they practice a little astrology with the Index of Leading Indicators. The index is made up of twelve statistics that tend to signal the coming of recessions and recoveries. These indicators include the supply of money and credit, total employment in manufacturing, retail and wholesale inventories, and even the number of companies reporting slower deliveries of goods. Though accurate to a degree, the index is far from perfect. If the index used today had been available since 1948, it would have predicted not only the six recessions that have occurred, but also two others that never materialized.

Liquidity — Firms control and own many valuable things: machinery, bonds, bank accounts, unfinished and finished products. Some of these assets are more *liquid* — more easily sold for cash with little or no risk — than others. Liquidity, the ability to safely sell valuables for cash, is important because firms need dollars in their day-to-day operations.

Monetary Policy — See *Stimulation.*

Multinational Firm — A firm that is predominately owned and controlled by capitalists in one country, but has factories, offices, and/or outlets in more than one country. Thus the firm does not just sell its products all over the world; it is directly involved in production and politics around the globe.

Nationalization — The transfer of ownership and control of specific firms from a private owner to the national government. The main motivation of a nationalized firm is not necessarily to make money; rather, it might operate to provide the cheapest and best service possible for a large part of the population. The goals and performance of a nationalized industry depend on who controls the government body that runs it.

Productivity — A favorite theme among businesses, productivity refers to workers' output and performance; it is a measure of the amount of goods produced divided by the time it took to produce them. Since more output could mean more profit, workers' productivity is constantly assessed by their employers. Means of boosting productivity — such as on-the-job speedup, management supervision and control over work, and automation — may be good for owners' incomes, but are not necessarily "profitable" for workers.

Profit — When you go to work, you get a wage. However, the dollar value of what you produce on the job is greater than your wage. Private property rights ensure that the person or firm that hired you gets the difference between the dollar value of your output and your wages. Some of the difference pays for the machinery, equipment, and raw materials; the rest is profit.

The shares going to wages and profits are not fixed; there is a continual struggle between workers and capitalists over the distribution of income from production.

Protection — Frequently, a government will choose to make it difficult for foreign businesses to sell certain goods within its territory. For example, in many nonindustrial nations, governments would like to limit imports in order to encourage domestic industry. Or special interest groups in a country may persuade the government to limit competition from imports. When the government chooses to limit imports, it is following a policy of protection — as opposed to free trade. One common form of protection is to charge a tax — or tariff — on imports. Another method of protection is to place quotas on certain imports.

Real Wages — Your real wage is the bundle of actual items you can purchase with your income. When firms are raising prices, your real wage can go down even though your wage in terms of dollars has risen. Real wages are often expressed in some past year's prices; throughout the 1970s, the base year most commonly used was 1967. Your wage expressed in 1967 dollars — your real wage — is the amount of money you needed in 1967 to buy what your wages buy today.

Recession — The "official" definition of recession is "a period of at least six months during which the amount of goods and services produced for sale declines." There are no exactly defined limits as to how bad things must get before a recession turns into a *depression,* a term associated with much more severe declines in production, employment, and profits. The choice of which word to use — recession or depression — is a political one.

Reserve Currency — When a country has a balance of payments surplus, it receives more foreign currency than it spends. The various different currencies a country obtains usually will be traded for one of the major stable currencies, and held in that form. (These holdings, or reserves, are spent when the country has a balance of payments deficit.)

The currencies in which nations hold these reserves are called reserve currencies; a currency that is relatively stable and in large supply. For many years, the dollar was the main reserve currency, which resulted in the big build-up of dollars held abroad. In the 1970s other currencies such as the German mark have grown in importance as reserve currencies.

Socialism — An economic organization of society in which all the people control both their own lives and the direction of their society because they control production. Public ownership and economic planning enable the masses of people to determine what is produced, how it is produced, and how the product is distributed. To ensure this, democratic decision-making processes must be developed and a secure level of material well-being must be provided to everyone.

Stimulation — When unemployment is high and the level of production of goods and services is low, the government looks for ways to encourage or stimulate production. It may use *fiscal policy* — buying things directly, making payments to people (for instance, welfare checks), or reducing taxes. All these measures are intended to increase the demand for goods and, therefore, the profitability of production. It may also use *monetary policy* — attempting to do the same thing by lowering the cost of borrowing; that is, the interest rate.

Stimulation is necessary to keep the economy out of recession or depression.

Stocks and the Stock Market — When business people need funds to start or expand a corporation, they sell stocks (or bonds). Buyers of the stocks obtain ownership of a portion of the company and receive dividend payments from the company's revenues. People interested in buying or selling stock go to stockbrokers, who then take these offers to a stock exchange. An investor in stocks speculates what a company's performance in the future will be; the trading of stocks at an exchange based on these investor expectations creates a market for stocks, or, the stock market.

HOW TO SURVIVE:
SOURCES AND
RESOURCES

The facts and analyses in this book are drawn from five years of research by members of the *Dollars & Sense* collective and many outside writers. A complete set of footnotes citing books, newspaper and magazine articles, government statistical sources, and interviews would be as long as the book. We're listing here a few major sources that deserve particular credit or that we would encourage readers to pursue.

More important, we are including resources that can help readers decide what to do next, resources for self-education and action around the major problems we've discussed. We've tried to include guides to both personal protection and collective action; in most cases they turn out to be one and the same.

Work

Sources:

On the effect of scientific management and mechanization of work, see Harry Braverman's *Labor & Monopoly Capital: The Degradation of Work in the Twentieth Century,* (New York: Monthly Review Press, 1974). The coal mining interview that opens chapter one was conducted by Liberation News Service (LNS), which is an alternative weekly news service published in New York. News packets also include graphics and photos. Subscriptions are $20 a month; $240 per year. Write LNS at 17 West 17th Street, New York NY 10011.

Resources:

Legal protection against workplace hazards, to the extent that it exists, is available under the provisions of the Occupational Safety and Health Act of 1970, administered by the Occupational Safety and Health Administration. The more public pressure that can be brought to bear on OSHA, the better the chances are for the federal agency's action and enforcement of the regulations.

The best guides to using OSHA and finding workplace hazards are published by local branches of a group called the Committee on Safety and Health (COSH). COSH has a national network in cities and states that publishes materials and disseminates information on a variety of workplace hazards and how employees can best use existing laws. Two examples are: *How to Use OSHA*, a worker's guide to the agency, what the laws are, who is protected, and how to get OSHA to respond; and *How to Look at Your Workplace*, which tells you how to find workplace dangers, tests that can be made to prove the existence of these dangers, what unions can do about them, and what to do if there is no union in your workplace. (This pamphlet is available in both English and Spanish.) For a bibliography, price list, and the name of a COSH group in your area, write: Urban Planning Aid, MCOSH group, 123 Boylston Street, Boston MA 02116.

For another good up-to-date resource on health and safety issues write to *Monitor* (a monthly newsletter put out by the Industrial Commission of Ohio's Division of Occupational Safety and Hygiene); 246 North High Street, Columbus OH 43215.

A good guide to forming and using unions and on your rights as a worker is *Labor Law for the Rank and Filer* by Staughton Lynd, published (as a Singlejack Little Book) by Miles and Weir, Ltd.; Box 1906, San Pedro, CA 90733. They have a catalogue of other worker-related publications as well.

For more information about workers' rights and unionization, making work more meaningful, and organizing cooperative workplaces, contact: Vocations for Social Change, 107 South Street, Boston, MA 02111. They publish two booklets on unions and workers' rights: *Your Rights as a Worker (With a Special Section for Massachusetts Workers)* includes rights for employees under the federal labor laws, covering race and sex discrimination. *Choosing a Union* explains the best things about many unions: how democratic they are, which ones cover which workers, how to contact them, and so on.

Vocations for Social Change (see above) publishes an extensive guide on forming working cooperatives, *No Bosses Here: A Manual on Working Collectively*.

Unemployment

Sources:

A detailed history of the Employment Act of 1946 can be found in Stephen K. Bailey, *Congress Makes a Law*, Columbia University Press, 1950.

Resources:

Many local groups offer advice and support for people seeking unemployment compensation; specific regulations vary from state to state, but for information on how to set up an unemployment compensation counseling service contact Vocations for Social Change (see under Work for address). Likewise there are local organizing efforts in many cities among both unemployed workers and employees of CETA and other government jobs programs; a national organization in touch with many of these efforts is Jobs & Justice, 1605 Connecticut Ave., NW, Washington, D.C. 20009.

Labor and community groups in several states have introduced legislation to limit companies' ability to shut down local plants and move out of state; for information on the most advanced of these campaigns, contact: Ohio Public Interest Campaign, 340 Chester, 12th Building, Cleveland OH 44414.

Women and the Family

Sources:

For material on women's role in the workforce see *Monthly Review*, July–August 1976. Two articles are useful in this issue: "The Working Class Has Two Sexes," by Rosalyn Baxandall, Elizabeth Ewen, and Linda Gordon; and "The Other Side of the Paycheck," by Batya Weinbaum. For details on women's entrance into and expulsion from heavy industry during and after World War II, see William Chafe's *The American Woman: Her Changing Social, Economic, and Political Roles, 1920–1970* (New York: Oxford University Press, 1972). The Winter 1977–78 issue of *Radical America* contains a good article on the family and the new political Right, "Sex, Family, and the New Right: Anti-Feminism as a Political Force," by Linda Gordon and Allen Hunter. Reprints are available from *Radical America* (see under Socialism for address).

Resources:

Women in the paid workforce, especially clerical workers, are increasingly creating their own unions, caucuses, and organizations. See Jean Tepperman's *Not Servants, Not Machines: Office Workers Speak Out!* (Boston: Beacon Press, 1976). On the national level, contact: Working Women, 1258 Euclid, Cleveland OH 44115, which can put you in touch with local clerical workers' groups.

Outside the workplace, a lot of action on women's roles and rights focuses on reproductive rights and the Equal Rights Amendment. For information on what's being done on the legislative level on the issue of abortion rights, contact: National Abortion Rights Action League (NARAL), 825 15th Street NW, Washington, D.C. 20005. For more direct involvement in political action centering around abortion and sterilization abuse issues, contact: Reproductive Rights National Network, 3244 N. Clark Street, Chicago, IL 60657.

The National Organization for Women (NOW) is the most active group working for the Equal Rights Amendment (ERA). They have many state and local offices, but their national office is at 425 13th Street, NW, Suite 1048, Washington, D.C. 20004.

For a well-researched, reliable, and up-to-date analysis of these and other current women's issues see *Off Our Backs*, a monthly women's journal. The address is: 1724 20th Street, NW, Washington, D.C. 20009.

Government

Resources:

The Conference/Alternative State and Local Public Policies, 1901 Q Street, NW, Washington, D.C. 20009, is a clearinghouse for state and local reform legislation and campaigns. Their publications include resource lists on local organizations and activities, as well as a just-published guide to local organizing approaches centering on taxes, housing, utilities, and other issues.

For tax reform information on the federal level, contact Tax Reform Research Group, PO Box 14198, Washington, D.C. 20044; their monthly bulletin *People and Taxes* is $7.50 a year for individuals; the manual *Tax Politics: How They Make You Pay and What You Can Do About It* is $6.95 ($4.95 with a subscription to *People & Taxes*).

Two groups campaigning for cuts in the military budget and increased funding for human needs are Coalition for a New Foreign and Military Policy, 120 Maryland Ave., NE, Washington, D.C. 20002; and Mobilization for Survival, 3601 Locust Walk, Philadelphia, PA 19104.

Monopolies and Energy

Sources:

On the history of the international oil cartel, see: John M. Blair, *The Control of Oil* (New York: Random House, 1978). On the oil companies' role in nuclear power, see Anna Gyorgy and Friends, *No Nukes* (Boston: South End Press, 1979).

Resources:

A very readable, profusely illustrated educational material for use in work on monopolies and inflation is *Why Do We Spend So Much Money?*, published by Popular Economics Press, Box 221, Somerville, MA 02143. Most action centering on energy alternatives and against oil company and utility company plans is organized on a local or regional level. National coalitions and clearinghouses working for secure, affordable energy supplies and energy conservation include: Energy Action, 1523 L Street NW, Washington, D.C. 20005; and the Citizen-Labor Energy Coalition, 1300 Connecticut Avenue, Room 401, Washington, D.C. 20036 or 600 W. Fullerton, Chicago, IL 60614. National contacts for information on antinuclear activities are Nuclear Information and Resource Service, 1536 16th Street, NW, Washington, D.C. 20036; *Critical Mass Journal*, PO Box 1538, Washington, D.C. 20013; and Mobilization for Survival (see under Government for address).

World Food

Sources:

Much of the material in chapter six is based on the work of the Institute for Food and Development Policy. Their published materials include Frances Moore Lappé and Joseph Collins, *Food First: Beyond the Myth of Scarcity* (Boston: Houghton Mifflin, 1977).

Resources:

In this country, efforts to limit the power of and gain some independence from agribusiness include farming and food-buying cooperatives, land reform legislation, emergency food supply programs, union organizing, and nutrition education. These issues, as well as corporate and AID activities overseas, are regularly covered in *Food Monitor*, PO Box 1975, Garden City, NY 11530. Also contact Institute for Food and Development Policy, 2588 Mission Street, San Francisco, CA 94110. The most effective way to bring about a better use of the world's land is to push for an end to U.S. government support of right-wing regimes that maintain the power of agribusiness and local elites; contact Coalition for a New Foreign and Military Policy (see under Government for address).

Trade

Sources:

For information on Japan see: Jon Halliday, *A Political History of Japanese Capitalism* (New York: Monthly Review Press, 1978). Besides Blair's *The Control of Oil* (see under Monopolies and Energy), for analysis of the energy situation see: Joe Stork, *Middle East Oil and the Energy Crisis* (New York: Monthly Review Press, 1975).

An explanation of how the U.S. auto companies' production advantages declined can be found in Emma Rothchild, *Paradise Lost: The Decline of the Auto-Industrial Age,* (New York: Random House, 1974); see especially chapters six through eight.

Socialism

The following national periodicals offer socialist viewpoints on current news events and political organizing:

Seven Days (a biweekly news magazine); 206 Fifth Avenue, New York, NY 10010.

For weekly newspapers see: *The Guardian,* 33 W. 17th Street, New York, NY 10011; and *In These Times,* 1509 N. Milwaukee Avenue, Chicago, IL 60622.

Specialized magazines with a socialist perspective include:

Dollars & Sense (a monthly bulletin of economic affairs); 38 Union Square, Room 14, Somerville, MA 02143.

Monthly Review (reports on and analyzes current political and economic problems with a special emphasis on imperialism); 62 W. 14th Street, New York, NY 10011.

Radical America (an independent socialist and feminist bimonthly magazine published by a Boston-area collective of six men and six women); P.O. Box B, North Cambridge, MA 02140.

Science for the People (a monthly journal published by the group of the same name; reports on issues relating to science and technology and political organizing among technical and professional workers in those fields); *Science for the People*, 897 Main Street, Cambridge, MA 02139.

The Review of Radical Political Economics (published monthly by the Union for Radical Political Economics; includes theoretical and analytical articles on capitalism and socialism); 41 Union Square West, Room 901, New York, NY 10003.

INDEX

Accumulation, in capitalist system, 160
Affirmative action programs, 20–21
AFL-CIO, 15, 19, 38, 152
Africa, effects of French imperialism in, 110–115; U.S. aid to, 119
Agency for International Development (AID), 115–119
Agribusiness, in Sahel region of Africa, 113–115; and U.S. foreign aid policy, 115–119
Agriculture, effect of imperialism on, 108–110
Ahmed Zaki Yamani, 95
Alaska, unemployment in, 27
Aldrich, Winthrop, 37
Allende, Salvador, 119
Allied Chemical, 101–102
Amalgamated Clothing and Textile Workers Union, 18
Amax mining conglomerate, 98
American Collectors Association, 58
American Economic Review, 31
American Farm Bureau Federation, 39
American Federation of Labor and Congress of Industrial Organizations, *see* AFL-CIO
Anti-nuclear power groups, 147
Aramco, 91
Ashe, A. J., 88
Australia, grain trade of, 108
Auto industry, effect of foreign competition on, 130–131; monopoly in, 86, 87–88

B-1 bomber controversy, 80–81. *See also* Military spending
Balance of payments, U.S., 132, 133–136, 160
Balance of trade, U.S., 132–133, 134, 136; defined, 160–161; effect of dollar devaluation on, 137–138; effect of recession on, 139–140; *See also* International economics
Bank of America, 115
Banks, and urban fiscal crisis, 67–69
Banzer, General Hugo, 119
Beer industry, 84–85
Birth control, in poor countries, 118–119
Bituminous Coal Operators' Association, 9
Black lung disease, 68
Blacks, affirmative action programs for, 20–21; job discrimination against, 4–5, 20; median family income of, 22–23;

types of jobs held by, 21–22; unemployment rates for, 27–28
Blumenthal, W. Michael, 75, 138
Boston, and urban fiscal policy, 67; workers' collective action in, 5
Boyle, Tony, 8
Braverman, Harry, 12
Brazil, multinational firms' development of, 121–122
British East India Company, 110
British Petroleum (BP), 90, 91, *See also* Oil companies
Brookings Institution, 71, 72, 81
Brown, Donaldson, 39
Bryant, Anita, 59
Bud Antle, Inc., 113
Budget, national, 64–65. *See also* Government
Bud Senegal, 113–115
Bundy, McGeorge, 81
Bunge grain company, 109
Business, *see* Private business
Business cycle, causes of, 29–35; government's role in controlling, 73–78
Business Week, 69, 73, 75, 109, 131, 138

Canada, grain trade of, 108
Capital, defined, 161
Capital formation, 68–69
Capital gains, 73
Capitalism, 143–146, 161
Cardenal, Ernesto, 105–107
Cargill grain company, 109, 116
Carnegie, Andrew, 84, 132
Cartel, defined, 161. *See also* Monopoly; Oil companies
Carter Administration, 26, 41, 72, 75, 80, 97, 102, 119, 139
Castle and Cooke, 114, 116, 120
Castro, Fidel, 155
CETA, 40
Chase Manhattan Bank, 44, 68
Chávez, Cesar, 113
Chevron, 90, 91, 146, involvement in coal industry, 98, 100; *See also* Oil companies
Child care services, 56–57
Chile, U.S. aid to, 119–120
Citibank, 68
Cities, fiscal crisis of, 66–69
Civil rights movement, 20, 65–66, 152
Civil Works Administration (CWA), 36–37

175

Class, defined, 161-162
Clerical workers, effect of productivity
    boosters on, 12-14; and unionization, 51,
    52; women employed as, 46, 47, 48, 50;
    workplace hazards for, 4
Cleveland, fiscal crisis in, 69
Clifford, Clark, 81
Coal, as alternative energy source, 98-100.
    See also Energy industry
Coal Mine Health and Safety Act, 8
Coal miners' strike, 5-10
Colcord, Lincoln, 36
Cold War, 78
Collins, Joseph, 113
Colonialism, see Imperialism
Committee for Action on Latin America,
    119
Committee for Economic Development
    (CED), 39
Communism, 153
Competition, see Foreign competition
Comprehensive Employment and Training
    Act (CETA), 40
Computerized offices, 12-14
Concentration, defined, 162
Congress of Industrial Organizations (CIO),
    152. See also AFL-CIO
Consolidation Coal, 98
Construction industry, effect of high unem-
    ployment on, 32; unionization in, 15, 16
Consumerism, of family, 53-54, 57-58
Continental grain company, 109
Continental Oil, 98, 100, 101. See also Oil
    companies
Continuous Miner, 7, 8
Corporations, see Multinational corporations;
    Private business
Council of Economic Advisors, 40
Council of Energy-Rich Tribes (CERT).,
    99-100
Crawford, Frederick, 49
Credit, consumer, 57-58
Cuba, socialist government in, 154; con-
    sciousness of, 157-158; decision making
    in, 155; economic security in, 155-156;
    personal choice in, 157; services of,
    156-157
Cuban Women's Federation, 155
Currency exchange rates, 134-136,
    162-163. See also Devaluation

Day-care services, 56-57
Debt, consumer, 57-58; public, 74
Deficit spending, of U.S. government,
    64-65, 71, 74, 162
Demand, effective, 33

Democratic Party, support of unions, 18-19
Deregulation, of natural gas prices, 95-96;
    of oil prices, 97
Devaluation, of U.S. dollar, 135, 162; effect
    on balance of trade, 137-138; and infla-
    tion, 138; and recession, 139-140
District of Columbia, unemployment in, 27
Divorce rates, 58-59
Dole Pineapple, 114, 120
Dollars & Sense collective, 148
Dow Chemical, 71
Dreyfus grain company, 109

Economic Report of the President, 40
Education, government spending on, 65
Eisenhower Administration, 26
Emergency Financial Control Board, 67
Employee-owned companies, 149-151
Employment Act, of 1946, 39
Energy crisis, 97; causes of natural gas
    shortage, 95-96; causes of oil shortage,
    92-95, 96-97; See also Oil companies
Energy industry, 89; coal, 98-100; nuclear
    power, 100-102; oil, 90-97; solar power,
    102-104
Environmental Protection Agency (EPA), 5
Equal Employment Opportunity Commis-
    sion, 20
Equal Opportunity and Full Employment
    Act, of 1975, 40-41
Exchange rates, currency, 134-136,
    162-163. See also Devaluation
Exxon, 89, 90, 91, 95; involvement in coal
    industry, 98, 99; solar power research of,
    102; uranium milling of, 100-101; See
    also Oil companies

Face the Nation, 95
Factory workers, 11-12. See also Manufac-
    turing industry
Family structure, changing, 46, 58-59;
    political movements supporting traditional,
    59-60; women's role in, 42-45
Fantus Corporation, 17
Federal Emergency Relief Administration, 36
Federal Power Commission, 95
Federal Reserve Banks, 74
Federal Reserve Board, 75
Federal Trade Commission, 86
Firestone Tire, 146
First National City Bank, 69
Fiscal policy, government, 73-75, 81, 166
Fixed exchange rate, of U.S. dollar, 135,
    162-163
Floating exchange rates, 135, 163
Food First (Lappé, Collins), 113, 115

Ford, Gerald, 80
Ford Motor Company, 71
Foreign aid, U.S., to Third World countries, 115–120
Foreign competition, rise in, 127–129; U.S. response to, 130–131
Foreign investment, U.S., 129–130
Foreign trade, U.S., 129, 130; balance of, 132–133, 134, 136; effect of devaluation of dollar on, 137–138; effect of recession on, 139–140; and trade negotiations, 139; See also International economics
Fortune, 20, 32, 75
French imperialism, in Africa, 111–115
Friedman, Milton, 71
Full Employment Act, 38
Full Employment and Balanced Growth Act, of 1976, 41

Garvin, Clifton, 95
General Electric, 12
General Motors, 17, 146
Getty Oil, 101. See also Oil companies
Government, employment programs of, 35–41; military budget of, 78–81; role in controlling business cycle, 73–78; spending trends of, 63–66, 81, 146; tax revolt against, 69–73; urban fiscal crisis of, 66–69; See also Foreign trade; International economics
Government workers, 16, 64; unionization of, 16, 17
Grain trade, 108–109
Great Depression, 26, 29, 65, 89; unemployment during, 26; unionism during, 15
Gross National Product, 34, 63–64, 69; indications of, 142–143, 163
Gulf, 90, 95; involvement in coal industry, 98; involvement in nuclear power industry, 100, 101–102; solar power research of, 102; See also Oil companies

Hamilton, Allan, 92
Hartmann, Heidi, 53
Hawkins, Augustus, 40
Health hazards, see Occupational health hazards
Health insurance, national, 19, 63
Health programs, government spending on, 65–66, 181
Highway construction, government spending on, 64, 65, 146
Hispanic peoples, see Nonwhites
Hopkins, Harry, 36
Housework, as unpaid labor, 43–44. See also Women's work

Humphrey-Hawkins Bill, 40–41
Hunger, world, estimates of, 108
Hyde, Henry, 59, 60

IBM, 13, 14, 50
Imperialism, 107–108, 163; effect on world agriculture, 108–110; of multinational corporations, 120–122; in Sahel countries of Africa, 110–115; and U.S. foreign aid programs, 115–119
Indian Affairs, Bureau of, 100
Indian resistance, to energy companies, 99–100, 101
Industrial Workers of the World, 152
Industrias Amolonca, 116
Inflation, 163–164; and devaluation of dollar, 138; effect on foreign trade, 137; effect of monopolization on, 86–89; private industry's reaction to, 33–34; and unemployment, 76–77
Injury, see Occupation health hazards
Interest rates, effects of high, 139–140. See also Monetary policy
International economics, indicators of U.S. decline in, 132–136; reasons for U.S. decline in, 129–132; rise of competition in, 127–129; U.S. response for improving position in, 136–141; See also Foreign trade
Investment, see Foreign investment
Iranian oil, 91, 93, 96. See also Oil companies
Island Creek Coal, 98

Japan, economic development since WWII, 127, 128–129; trade negotiations with, 139; U.S. balance of trade with, 134, 140
Jarvis, Howard, 60, 70
Job discrimination, racial, 20–21; related to health hazards, 4–5
Job programs, government, 36–41
John Birch Society, 59–60
Johnson Administration, 79
Joint Economic Committee of Congress, 88, 95
Journal of Home Economics, 55
J. P. Stevens, 18, 19

Kellner, Irwin, 51
Kerr-McGee, 100
Keystone Coal Industry Manual, 98
Kinder-Care Learning Centers, Inc., 56
Kroc, Ray, 54

Labor Department, 26, 27

Labor and Monopoly Capital (Braverman), 12
Labor-saving goods, for home, 54–55
Labor Statistics, Bureau of, 3, 4, 79
Labor unions, see Union membership
Ladies' Home Journal, 48
Lappé, Frances, Moore, 113
Latin American Agribusiness Development Corporation (LAAD), 115–116
Leading indicators, defined, 164
Lead poisoning, job-related, 4, 5
Lee, Ivy, 90
Liquidity, defined, 164
Loose money policy, 74
Lung disease, job-related, 4

Machine operators, 12, 46; women employed as, 47
Machinery and Allied Products Institute, 39
Manufacturing industry, 11–12, 16; employment of nonwhites in, 21, 22; monopolies in, 84–86; runaway shops in, 17–18, 19; unionization in, 15, 16, 21; women employed in, 49–50
Marcos, President Ferdinand, 119
Meany, George, 15
Mechanization, 10–11, 29; in coal mining industry, 6–8; effect on housework, 54–55; of foreign firms, 130–131; for office work, 12–14
Median income, black vs. white, 22–23; women's, 46, 52–53
Medicaid, 65–66
Medical benefits, coal miners', 6, 7, 9, 10
Medicare, 65–66
Mexican oil, 97. See also Oil companies
Michigan Taxpayers United, 71
Middle Eastern oil, and OPEC, 92–95, 97; and Seven Sisters, 91; See also Oil companies, OPEC
Military spending, of government, 64, 65, 78–81
Miller, Arnold, 8, 9
Miller, G. William, 75
Miller (brewery), 84–85
Miners for Democracy movement, 9
Mining industry, strikes of, 5–10; unionization of, 15, 16
Mobil, 90, 91, 95; solar power interests of, 102; See also Oil companies
Mobuto Sese Seko, General, 119
Monetary policy, government, 74–75, 139–140, 166–167
Monopoly, 84–86; history of oil companies', 90–97; and long-run inflation, 86–89; See also Oil companies

Morgan, Marabel, 59
Multinational corporations, 78, 164; in Third World countries, 113–115, 120–122
Municipal Assistance Corporation, 67
Municipal employment, and fiscal crisis, 66, 67–68
Murray, James, 38

Nader, Ralph, 131
National Association of Manufacturers (NAM), 38, 49
National defense, see Military spending
National Farmers Union, 38
National Institute of Health, 79
Nationalization, of industry, 151–152, 164–165. See also Socialism
National Labor Relations Act, 19
National Labor Relations Board, 18
National Manpower Institute's National Commission on Working Women, 46, 55
National Tax Limitation Committee (NTLC), 70
Natural gas, shortage of, 95–96
Natural Gas Act, of 1978, 96
New Deal, 18, 36–37
Newsweek, 51
New York, fiscal crisis in, 67; unemployment in, 27, 28
New York Times, 6
Nicaragua, agribusiness in, 116
Niskanen, William, 71
Noise, as workplace hazard, 4, 5
Nonwhites, types of jobs held by, 21–23; unemployment rates of, 27–28; See also Blacks
Nooter, Robert, 116
Not Servants, Not Machines: Office Workers Speak Out (Tepperman), 13
Nuclear power, as alternative energy source, 100–102, See also Energy Industry
Nurses, women employed as, 46, 47
Nursing home industry, 66

Oakley, Anne, 43
Occidental Petroleum, 98
Occupational health hazards, 3–5; in coal mining industry, 5, 7–8; in steel industry, 11; in uranium mining industry, 101
Occupational Safety and Health Administration (OSHA), 5
Office workers, see Clerical workers
Oil companies, buying of coal resources, 98–100; events causing price-increases of, 92–95, 96–97; and independent competition, 91–92, 93–94; and natural gas shortage, 95–96; nuclear power invest-

ments of, 100–102; Seven Sisters cartel of, 90–91; solar power interests of, 102–104

Oligopoly, 86. *See also* Monopoly

O'Neal, Ed, 39

OPEC (Organization of Petroleum Exporting Countries), 91–95, 97; effect of U.S. dollar devaluation on, 138; U.S. balance of payments with, 136

OSHA, *see* Occupational Safety and Health Administration

Overproduction, and unemployment, 33

Panic of 1837, 29

Part-time workers, and unemployment rates, 26, 27; women as, 51

Peabody coal company, 98

Penn Mutual Life Insurance, 14

Pepsico, Inc., 85

Philip Morris, 84

Philippines, U.S. aid to, 120

Phillips (natural gas producer), 95

Population control, in poor countries, 118–119

Price controls, for fighting inflation, 77

Prices, monopolies' control of, 87–89

Private business, government policies for stimulating, 73–78; government spending to stimulate, 64–65; opposition to government job programs, 36–41; profit-motivated cycle of, 28–35, 74; tax revolt of, 70–71; and urban fiscal crisis, 67–69

Productivity, in clerical work, 12–14; defined, 165; effect of high unemployment on, 30–35; industry's goal of higher, 6–7, 10–11; and workplace health, 6–7, 11

Professionals, 12; nonwhites employed as, 21–22; women employed as, 46–47

Profit, defined, 165; and fluctuations in business cycle, 28–35

Proposition 13, 70, 72

Protectionism, 139, 165

Public Interest Research Group (PIRG), 79

Puerto Rico, sterilization programs in, 118–119

Ralston Purina, 116

Ravenholt, Dr. R. T., 118

Real wages, defined, 165–166; *See also* Wages

Recession, causes of, 30–35, 74; defined, 29–30, 166; effect on balance of trade, 139–140; government's role in, 74–77

Recovery, in business cycle, 34–35

Research and development, government spending on, 64

Reserve currency, U.S. dollar as, 135–136, 166

Retail trade industry, 16; unionization of, 16, 17; women employed in, 47–48, 50

"Right-to-work" laws, 17, 18

Rockefeller, David, 80

Rockefeller, John D., 90, 103

Roosevelt, Franklin D., 29, 36, 38

Royal Dutch Shell, 90; involvement in nuclear power industry, 100, 101–102; *See also* Oil companies

Runaway shops, 17–18, 19, 29; international, 120–122

Safety measures, coal miners' strike for, 5–10

Sahel region, of Africa, imperialist development of, 110–115

St. Louis Post-Dispatch, 118

Sales, *see* Retail trade industry

São Paulo, Brazil, auto strikes in, 122

Saudi Arabian oil, 91, 93, 97. *See also* Oil companies, OPEC

Scali, John, 109

Schlafly, Phyllis, 59

Scientific management, for increased productivity, 10, 12

Sears Roebuck, 37

Secretarial workers, *see* Clerical workers

Selective Service Act, 49

Senate Committee on Energy and Natural Resources, 98

Senate Foreign Relations Committee, 91

Service workers, 11–12, 16; unionization of, 16; women employed as, 46, 47, 50, 51

Seven Sisters, 90, 91. *See also* Oil companies

Sexism, of unions, 52

Skin disorders, job-related, 4

Skinner, Elliot, 112

Socialism, 148–149, 151–154, 166; in Cuba, 154–159; and worker-owned companies, 149–151

Social services, government spending for, 65–66, 81; and urban fiscal crisis, 68, 69

Solar power, as alternative energy source, 102–104. *See also* Energy industry

Somoza, Anastasio, 106, 107

Southern U.S., industrial growth of, 17–18

Stagflation, 76–77

Standard of California, *see* Chevron

Standard of New Jersey, *see* Exxon

Standard of New York, *see* Mobil

Standard Oil Trust, 90. *See also* Oil companies

Steel industry, effect of foreign competition

on, 131; increased productivity in, 11

Sterns, Reverend F., 42–43, 44, 59

Stimulation of economy, government, 64–65, 73–75, 166–167

Stock market, 167

Strikes, coal miners, 5–10; effect of high unemployment on, 31–32

Strip mining, 7–8, 99

Tanner, Alice, 18

Tariffs, effects of, 139

Tax burden, distribution of, 71–73

Tax revolt, of business, 70–71; and effectiveness of reforms, 71–73; of public sector, 69–70

Teachers, women employed as, 46, 47

Teamsters, 15

Technical workers, 11, 12; women employed as, 47

Teen-agers, unemployment rate of, 27–28

Tepperman, Jean, 13

Texaco, 90, 91, 95. See also Oil companies

Thailand, U.S. aid to, 120

Third World countries, and imperialism, 109–110; multinational corporations in, 112–115; U.S. aid programs to, 115–120

Tight money-policy, 74, 139–140

Tokyo Round, 139

Trade, see Balance of trade; Foreign trade

Transportation, in capitalist system, 145–146; government spending on, 64, 65, 81; in socialist system, 148–149

Tucker, Phil, 1–3

Unemployment, for black college graduates, 22; causes of, 28–35; effect on wages, 30–32; government's role in coping with, 35–41; and increased productivity, 7, 11, 13, 14; and inflation, 76–77; official rates of, 26–28; women and, 50–51

Union membership, decreasing, 15–20; lack of women in, 51–52

United Auto Workers, 4, 5, 86

United Electrical Workers, 5

United Farm Workers, 113

United Mine Workers, 5–10, 99

United States, foreign aid policy of, 115–120; grain trade of, 108–109; See also International economics

Unsafe at Any Speed (Nader), 131

Uranium mining, 100–101

Urban fiscal crisis, 66–69

U.S. News & World Report, 9

U.S. Steel, 11

Van Buren, Pres. Martin, 29

Vanderlip, Frank A., 37

Venezuelan oil, 91. See also Oil companies

Vermont Asbestos Group (VAG), 150–151

Vietnam War, 70, 79, 80, 81, 152; effect on U.S. position in international economics, 133, 135

Volkswagen, history of, 123–126; in Third World countries, 121, 122

Wages, coal miners', 7, 8–9; effect of high unemployment on, 30–32; increases of, for fighting inflation, 77; real, 27, 165–166; women's, 46, 48, 50, 51, 52–53

Wall Street Journal, 68, 75, 88

Watergate, 70

West Germany, economic development of, since WWII, 127–128, 133; U.S. balance of trade with, 134, 140

Wholesale trade industry, 16

Wildcat strikes, 6, 8

Women, job discrimination against, 4–5, 13; unemployment rate for, 27

Women's Bureau, Labor Department, 49

Women's liberation movement, 152

Women's work, in home 42–45, 53; and child care services, 56–57; and home consumption, 53–54, 58; and labor-saving goods, 54–55; political movements supporting traditional, 59–60; shopping and consumer credit, 57–58

Women's work, outside home, 44, 44–45; history of, 47–50; lack of unionization for, 51–52; percentages on, 45–46; types of, 46–47; and unemployment, 50–51; wages for, 46, 48, 50, 51, 52–53

Wood, Robert, 37

Woodcock, Leonard, 4

Word Processing, 14

Word-processing systems, 13–14

Workplace health, see Occupational health hazards

Works Progress Administration (WPA), 37

World Bank, 108, 114

World War II, 29, 37; rise of foreign competition since, 127–129; and unionism, 15; U.S. overseas spending after, 133; women in workforce during, 48–50

Xerox, 13

Yablonski, Jock, 8